Great Meals
IN MINUTES

PICNIC &
OUTDOOR
MENUS

TIME
LIFE
BOOKS

TIME-LIFE BOOKS, ALEXANDRIA, VIRGINIA

Contents

MEET THE COOKS 4

PICNIC & OUTDOOR MENUS IN MINUTES 7

PANTRY 16

EQUIPMENT 18

JANE UETZ 20

Oriental Chicken and Rice Salad / Chinese Cabbage, Snow Peas, and Cucumber
Pineapple with Orange-Chocolate Sauce 22

Butterflied Leg of Lamb with Savory Sauce
Stir-Fried Zucchini and Yellow Squash / Fresh Mint and Watercress Salad 24

Monterey Beef Roast / Roast Potatoes with Herbed Butter
Carrot and Broccoli Salad 26

ROBERTA RALL 28

Grilled Cornish Hens with Oriental Flavors / Stir-Fried Carrots with Snow Peas
Fresh Fruit in Cookie Cups 30

Grilled Monkfish with Lime-Butter Baste
Marinated Vegetables / Bulgur with Carrots and Scallions 32

Great Grilled Burgers / Raw Vegetables with Creamy Basil Dip
Fruit Layers with Vanilla Sauce 34

RON DAVIS 36

Duck, Chicken, and Veal Salad
Pasta with Three Cheeses / Asparagus with Garlic Dressing 38

Grilled Bluefish with Spinach, Bread, and Vegetable Stuffing
Tomato, Onion, and Arugula Salad / Leeks with Roasted Pepper and Bûcheron Cheese 40

Scallop Seviche
Sweet-and-Spicy Barbecued Spareribs / Honey-Mustard Coleslaw 44

VICTORIA WISE 48

Salmon Barbecued with Fennel, Lemon, and Onion
Grilled Corn / Cucumbers and Radishes with Watercress 50

Grilled Rabbit / Grilled Yellow and Green Bell Peppers
Mediterranean Tomato Salad 52

Pork Loin Roasted with Garlic and Sage
Artichokes Oreganata / Tapénade 54

BRUCE CLIBORNE 56

Mesquite-Grilled Clams, Oysters, and Lobsters
Herbed New Potatoes, Carrots, and Scallions / Cucumbers and Tomatoes with Lime   58

Grilled Loin of Pork with Fresh Thyme / Marinated Corn Salad
Sweet-and-Sour Peaches and Plums   60

Sea Scallops with Herbed Crème Fraîche / Poached Fennel
Orange, Radish, and Coriander Salad   64

NICHOLAS BAXTER 66

Loin of Lamb with Tomato and Mushroom Stuffing
Watercress and Hazelnut Salad / Orzo with Sour Cream and Black Pepper   68

Grilled Salmon Steaks with Fresh Dill and Thyme
Mélange of Fresh Vegetables   70

Loin of Veal Poached with Vegetables in White Wine
Wild Rice with Red Pepper and Cassis   72

FRANK BAILEY 74

Spinach Pâté
Pasta Salad with Pesto / Cold Orange Duck   76

Chilled Cream of Tomato Soup with Tequila
Fajitas / Spanish Rice Salad   78

Grilled Shrimp with Butter Sauce
Grilled Baked Fish / Roasted Pepper Salad   80

JOHN RISSER 82

Marinated Chicken Breasts / Potato Salad Vichyssoise
Mushroom and Cauliflower Salad   84

Barbecued Beef Kabobs
Tomatoes with Goat Cheese / Cucumber and Grapefruit Salad   86

Grilled Stuffed Lamb Chops
Mixed Bean Salad / Cheese and Fruit Medallions   88

VICTORIA FAHEY 90

Eggplant Salad / Falafel
Hummus / Cucumber Salad   92

Glazed Ham
Picnic Bread with Assorted Cheeses / Apple-Apricot Chutney   94

Spinach and Potato Soup
Herbed Roast Turkey Legs / Pumpkin-Corn Muffins   98

ACKNOWLEDGMENTS 101   INDEX 101

Meet the Cooks

JANE UETZ

Jane Uetz began her cooking career in the test kitchens of a major food company in New York City. She later joined the staff of *American Home* magazine as Associate Food Editor. Presently she is the director of the consumer and culinary center of a New York public relations agency. She also teaches cooking classes for business executives and appears on television and radio as a food and nutrition specialist.

ROBERTA RALL

Roberta Rall works as a free-lance food stylist and home economist. As such, she prepares and styles food for photography for numerous publications, including cookbooks and publicity releases; develops recipes for specific food products and audiences; and organizes taste tests. She has contributed food articles to *Women's World Magazine* and *Weight Watchers® Magazine*.

RON DAVIS

For three generations, Ron Davis' family have been professional cooks, so he comes by his love of cooking naturally. In 1978, he moved from Pennsylvania to New York and is now co-owner of the Washington Street Cafe as well as the Washington Street Cafe Caterers, both in New York City. He is head chef for the catering company.

VICTORIA WISE

Victoria Wise, a self-taught cook, has been cooking professionally since 1971, when she left her graduate studies in philosophy to become the first chef at Berkeley's Chez Panisse, a restaurant well known to U.S. gastronomes. She left Chez Panisse in 1973 to start her own charcuterie, called Pig by the Tail Charcuterie, in Berkeley, California.

BRUCE CLIBORNE

Chef, food stylist, recipe developer, and caterer Bruce Cliborne experiments with elements of every kind of cuisine. A native Virginian, he moved to New York, and began to work in restaurants; he has now been dinner chef at the Soho Charcuterie for several years and has taught at the New School for Social Research. Bruce Cliborne was a contributing author of and food stylist for the *Soho Charcuterie Cookbook*.

NICHOLAS BAXTER

The son of an English diplomat, Nicholas Baxter describes himself as a restaurateur-caterer by instinct. After studying finance, he later apprenticed at the Café Royal in London. Then, he worked as a waiter, maître d', and manager of various restaurants in London and the Caribbean. Now living in New York, Nicholas Baxter has worked with Manhattan caterer Donald Bruce White. Presently, he owns his own catering firm, Nicholas Baxter & Co., Ltd.

FRANK BAILEY

As partner in two New Orleans restaurants and their affiliated catering service, Frank Bailey specializes in serving fresh Louisiana ingredients. He has written extensively about food, wine, and travel for various publications and is the food columnist for *The Times Picayune/The States Item* of New Orleans. He is also technical consultant for the television series, The Great Chefs of New Orleans.

JOHN RISSER

John Risser grew up in a family of Pennsylvania-Dutch cooks and, as a child, learned how to appreciate and to prepare fine meals. As a professional cook, he has worked at Glorious Food, a New York City catering firm. In 1982, John Risser and two partners founded Chelsea Foods, a combination of food store, caterer, and café in New York City.

VICTORIA FAHEY

Californian Victoria Fahey, a self-taught cook, develops recipes and plans menus for an Oakland specialty food store, Charcuterie, and runs a catering service called Curds & Whey. She is also in charge of product development for a wholesaler of specialty foods, The New Oakland Food Company. She has contributed recipes to the *California Seafood Cookbook* and the *Bon Appetit Appetizers* book and is also a beekeeper.

Picnic & Outdoor Menus in Minutes
GREAT MEALS FOR FOUR, IN AN HOUR OR LESS

Picnics and barbecues, in one form or another, have been around for as long as mankind. A picnic is a communal meal most often eaten outdoors. A barbecue refers to a particular cooking method: the grilling of food (whole or in pieces, spitted or on a rack) over an open fire or directly on hot coals. But, in a social context, the distinction between the two blurs, for the terms *picnic* and *barbecue* are often synonymous. Both connote a style of entertaining, as informal or elaborate as the host chooses. Both can be enjoyed almost anywhere, at any time.

The term *barbecue*, most scholars agree, came from the Caribbean, from the Spanish or Arawak Indian word *barbacoa*. The Arawak's *barbacoa* was a latticework screen of green sticks on which meat was cooked over a fire. As Spanish conquistadores traveled to North America from the Caribbean, they probably brought the word with them. Although the word *picnic* only entered the English language in the mid-1700s, the first European picnickers in North America were the Pilgrims in 1621. To accommodate an unexpectedly large turnout of Indian guests, they held their three-day Thanksgiving feast outdoors. Early American picnics were called "frolics." As the name suggests, guests indulged in games, listened to musicians, and ate well. By the mid-1800s, Americans picnicked to celebrate any number of social events, particularly the Fourth of July. As testimony to American eating habits, an English traveler in 1870 noted that "picnics are going off in every direction—quiet little church picnics, Sunday school picnics, social picnics, work people's picnics, Fenian picnics, picnics of a hundred societies and associations."

Today, an American picnic can mean almost any meal, including a clambake, fish fry, hiking-trail snack, tailgate repast, and, of course, a barbecue. In fact, since America's post-World War II shift to suburbia, barbecuing has reached boom proportions and is now a national summer pastime. Cheap fuel (such as charcoal briquettes), many varieties of convenient, sturdy grills, and handy barbecuing accessories (see page 14) have furthered its popularity.

Skewered cubes of meat and slices of red and green bell peppers grill over charcoal for this feast. On the table are all the makings and equipment for a successful outdoor meal (clockwise, from top left): a metal ice chest, sliced watermelon, a napkin-lined basket with loaves of bread, fruits and vegetables, and wine. The carryall basket on the bench is filled with tableware and cooking utensils.

On the following pages, nine of America's most talented cooks present 27 complete menus featuring picnics and barbecues. Every menu can be made in an hour or less, and the cooks focus on a new kind of American cuisine that borrows ideas and techniques from around the world but also values American native traditions. They use fresh produce—no powdered sauces, canned soups, or other dubious shortcuts. Additional ingredients (vinegars, spices, herbs, and so on) are all high quality yet available for the most part in supermarkets or, occasionally, in a specialty shop. Each of the menus serves four people and includes ideas for planning and transporting outdoor meals.

The photographs accompanying each meal show exactly how the dishes will look when you serve them. The cooks and the test kitchen have planned the meals for appearance as well as taste: The vegetables are brilliant and fresh, the visual combinations appetizing. The settings, whether for backyard or beach, feature brightly colored and attractive, but not necessarily expensive, serving pieces. You can readily adapt your own tableware to these menus in convenient ways that will please you and your guests.

For each menu, the Editors, with advice from the cooks, suggest wines and other beverages. And there are suggestions for the best uses of leftovers and for appropriate desserts. On each menu page, too, you will find a range of other tips, from the best way to shell shrimp to tricks for selecting the freshest produce. All the recipes have been tested meticulously to make sure that even a relatively inexperienced cook can complete them within the time limit. However, you may need to start the fire in advance, and be sure to leave enough time to chill certain picnic items. Packing up the meals and transporting them is also not included in the hour, but the cooking and assembling of the meals can be accomplished in an hour or less.

BEFORE YOU START
Great Meals in Minutes is designed for efficiency and ease. The books will work best for you when you follow these suggestions:

1. Read the guidelines (pages 8–13) for transporting food and for cooking outdoors, if you are barbecuing.

2. Refresh your memory on the few simple cooking techniques described on the following pages. They will quickly become second nature and will help you produce professional meals in minutes.

3. Read the menus *before* you shop. Each one opens

SAFETY NOTES

Perishables

▶ To inhibit bacterial growth, you must keep food cold, at 45°F or below. Perishable food allowed to sit at room temperature for even a short time in hot weather may cause food poisoning.

▶ Open the ice chest as infrequently as possible, and never let it stand open. If possible, keep the ice chest in a shady spot. Remove your food from the ice chest only as you need it. Never unpack your entire meal and leave it out in the sun.

▶ Carry mayonnaise in a lidded jar on ice, and mix it with other ingredients just before serving.

Outdoor Cooking

▶ Be cautious and vigilant when you cook outdoors. Wherever you barbecue, select the fire site carefully, away from trees, grass, or shrubs that might ignite from sparks. Locate the fire downwind from your guests to avoid smoke irritation. Set up your barbecue where guests or pets cannot accidentally knock it over.

▶ Never start a fire with gasoline or kerosene. Always use a starter manufactured specifically for starting a barbecue fire. These starters meet all safety regulations. During cooking, do not leave the starter can near the fire.

▶ Never add a starter or instant-starting coals to a fire that is already lit.

▶ Never leave any fire unattended. If you have to go indoors momentarily, deputize a guest or family member to keep an eye on the fire.

▶ Never barbecue in an enclosed area unless you have adequate ventilation. Only use a working fireplace if the flue is open. To barbecue in a garage, the door must be open.

▶ To prevent flare-ups, follow the outdoor cooking tips (page 12) and make sure the coals are at the gray-ash stage before you put any food on for cooking.

▶ To put out flare-ups, raise the cooking grid away from the fire; spread the coals out; put a cover on your barbecue; or spray the flare-up with water.

▶ To douse a potentially dangerous flare-up, keep a bucket of water, or sand, handy or cover the fire with baking soda.

▶ Be sure that you extinguish all fires after cooking. Before disposing of the coals, check that they are quite dead; they should be cold to the touch.

▶ Wear an apron to protect clothing from spattering grease.

▶ Keep pot holders and mitts close enough to be handy, but never hang them over the edge of the grill when the fire is lit. Similarly, do not wear loose clothing that could dangle into the fire.

Indoor Cooking

Cooking at high temperatures can be dangerous, but not if you follow a few simple steps:

▶ Water added to hot fat will always cause spattering. If possible, pat foods dry with a cloth or paper towels before you add them to the hot oil in a skillet.

▶ Lay the food in the pan gently, or the fat will certainly spatter.

▶ Be aware of your cooking environment. If you are boiling or steaming some foods while sautéing others, place the pots far enough apart so the water is unlikely to splash into the oil.

▶ Turn pot handles inward, toward the middle of the stove, so that you do not accidentally knock something over.

---

with a list of all the required ingredients, listed in the order you would expect to shop for them in the average supermarket. Check for those few you need to buy; many items will already be on your pantry shelf.

4. Check the equipment list on page 18. A good sharp knife or knives and pots and pans of the right shape and material are essential for making great meals in minutes. This may be the time to look critically at what you own and to plan to buy a few things. The right equipment can turn cooking from a necessity into a creative experience.

5. Get out everything you need before you start to cook: The lists at the beginning of each menu tell just what is required. To save effort, keep your ingredients close at hand and always store them in the same place so you can reach for them instinctively.

6. Take your meat, fish, and dairy products out of the refrigerator early enough for them to come to room temperature (60° F) and thereby cut cooking time.

7. Read the introduction to each menu to find out if it is a picnic or a barbecue. Most meals are partially cooked in the kitchen, so follow the start-to-finish steps to coordinate the indoor and outdoor cooking.

PICNICS

Proper picnic equipment can provide comfort, safety, and a pleasing presentation. Your equipment need not be costly, but a few basics, such as an ice chest or insulated bag, are essential if you plan to carry foods in a car and then let them sit under a tree or on the beach for an hour or two. For optimum convenience, collect a set of picnic equipment that you can store together in one place and use only for outdoor eating. The following list includes the equipment essentials and a few options.

Picnic Equipment

Tableware: Placemats or a tablecloth, paper napkins, flatware, plastic cups, paper or plastic plates, salt and pepper shakers, condiment containers, and long-handled serving spoons and forks. If you dislike disposable plates, buying unbreakable plates and serving pieces in bright colors would be a practical investment.

Tools: A bottle opener, a corkscrew, wide-mouth Thermoses® for chunky foods, standard Thermoses® for soups and drinks, an insect repellant, a blanket, plastic bags for cleanup, paper towels, and a collapsible plastic jug for drinking water.

Carrying container: Wicker baskets or hampers are traditional but, because they are not insulated, will not keep food cold or hot. Several fancy ones come outfitted with utensils, salt and pepper shakers, and plastic boxes for packing sandwiches or other easy-to-crush foods, but you can use any convenient carrier and ordinary plastic containers. Sturdy shopping bags, used doubled or lined with newspaper, are fine for lightweight carrying.

Ice chest or insulated bag: One of these is necessary to prevent food that needs to be chilled from spoiling. If you plan to picnic frequently, invest in a large metal insulated chest constructed to keep food cold for hours. Lightweight Styrofoam® ice chests and insulated plastic bags are inexpensive alternatives and do a good job of preserving foods. Whatever insulated container you have, you must use ice cubes in a plastic bag, frozen containers of refrigerant jel, or dry ice to keep it cool. The last must be wrapped in several layers of newspaper, then placed on top of your food so that the carbon dioxide, which is heavier than air, goes downward over the food. Another alternative is to make your own ice pack by freezing water in a plastic container. You can prechill Thermoses® by filling them with ice water.

Packing Picnics

Except for sauces, all picnic food in this volume is meant to be served either at room temperature (60° F) or chilled. You can bring nonperishable food to room temperature by carrying it to your picnic in a noninsulated carrying container. For cold food, be sure to chill it thoroughly in advance and to pack all perishables in an ice chest.

Foil is indispensable for wrapping up food. Foil keeps food fresh, protected, and insulated. The most practical size is 12-inch heavy-duty foil. To wrap food or containers for packing, place them on a sheet of foil, bring the edges together over the food, and fold down several times. Then fold up the short ends (see accompanying illustrations). For a beach picnic, use foil to line your picnic basket to keep sand out of the food.

Pack all sandwich fixings on ice in separate containers, and make your sandwiches at the picnic site. They will taste fresher and be far less likely to spoil. Carry washed and dried salad greens and salad dressing in separate containers and combine them just before serving, unless the recipe states otherwise.

Tape down any screw-top or other lidded containers to prevent leaks and to keep them from opening up. Label every package for ease in unpacking later. Pack your picnic for the sequence in which you will use it: put the food in first, the utensils next, and the tablecloth on top. Pack the container so there are no empty spaces; if that is not possible, fill the spaces with crumpled newspaper so that nothing will bang together and break.

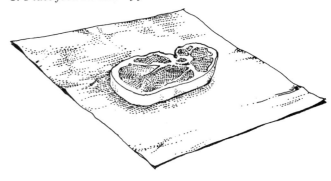

1. Place food on sheet of foil.

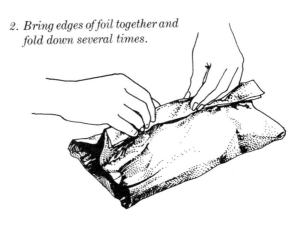

2. Bring edges of foil together and fold down several times.

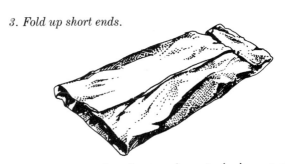

3. Fold up short ends.

Unless you are planning an elegant picnic, use plastic tumblers for beverages rather than your best crystal. If you must use breakable glassware, wrap each glass in several layers of kitchen towels or linen napkins and pack them in a separate carrying container. To keep wine chilled, pack bottles in your ice chest, or buy a lightweight insulated bag just for chilling wine.

BARBECUES

Barbecue equipment can be as simple or elaborate as you like. Basically, you need a container for the fire, a metal grid to hold the food over the fire, a small table or work surface near the grill, and long-handled cooking tools.

Grills

When selecting a barbecue grill, first decide how you intend to use it. Do you want it to be stationary or portable? Do you intend to cook for small groups or to entertain crowds? Will you be grilling steaks, chops, and hamburgers, or will you also want to cook large roasts? Where can you store the grill? If you have only a small balcony, you will have to consider a small unit.

Whatever you buy, the unit should be made from heavy-gauge metal, preferably with a porcelain enamel finish. This type of unit is sturdy enough to give you years of service, is easy to clean, and can be stored outdoors, although it should not be left out in the rain. The wires on the metal grid should be close enough to prevent food from falling through. As an option, you may want a barbecue with a hood or cover. This protects the fire from wind, and thus assures more even cooking. A hood can also accommodate an electric rotisserie, which is not called for in this volume. If your unit has legs, it should be well balanced.

Basic barbecuing units include:

Portable tabletop models: These are small enough to fit on a tabletop and ideal for picnics. They are available with or without dome-like covers. This category includes folding metal racks that fit over a campfire, cast-iron Japanese hibachis, and open braziers. Most portable grills are available in solid fuel (charcoal or wood) or gas models.

Portable tabletop grill

Standard-sized open braziers: These versatile uncovered grills, often on a tripod, are usually between 18 and 24 inches wide. Some braziers come equipped with a partial hood and a rotisserie, but usually lack a cover. Open braziers are available in solid fuel and gas models.

Open brazier

Covered cookers: These are available as round kettles, or square or rectangular free-standing grills. They should have a snug-fitting lid with an adjustable top vent. The vents in the bottom portion of the unit vary the air flow to the fire, allowing you to increase or decrease heat. The cover retains heat and protects the fire (letting you cook efficiently in inclement weather) and minimizes flame flare-up. Cooking with the cover on is similar to roasting in the oven; food rarely needs to be turned and cooks evenly. This method is also known as dry smoking. Without the cover, the unit cooks like a standard open brazier. Covered cookers are available in solid fuel, gas, and electric models.

Covered cooker

Stone barbecues and fire pits: Stone barbecues are permanent structures often found at picnic sites. You may use them for cooking the meals in this volume, but they lack the versatility and convenience of other barbecue units. Fire pits, such as Bruce Cliborne suggests for his Mesquite-Grilled Clams, Oysters, and Lobsters (see pages 58–59), are an even more primitive version of a barbecue unit.

Fuels

Several kinds of fuels are readily available, so your choice will depend on your grill model and preference.

Charcoal briquettes are an inexpensive fuel available nationwide. They ignite slowly and require the use of some type of firestarter. Briquettes are made from natural wood products that are pulverized and then mixed with other ingredients and pressed into a pillow shape. Charcoal made from hardwood is best. Briquettes are sold in 5-, 10-, and 20-pound bags. Also available are "instant starting" briquettes that are impregnated with kerosene. They catch fire quickly and are useful for cooking away from home. Never add starter briquettes to a lit fire. Charcoal briquettes were used for testing all recipes in this volume, except when the cook called for mesquite.

Wood is also a popular solid fuel. Hardwoods and fruit-woods, such a hickory, oak, birch, alder, ash, maple, and apple, are excellent for barbecuing because they produce long-lasting coals. Use soft woods for kindling only. Do not cook over resinous woods, such as pine, because they leave an unpleasant aftertaste on the food.

Another esteemed wood for barbecues is mesquite. A hard wood native to Texas, Arizona, and Northern Mexico, the Aztecs called it *mizquitl*, or "the honey tree." Mesquite is prized by cooks for the distinctive sweet, smoky taste it imparts to food. It ignites easily with any standard firestarter and has an intensely hot, long-lasting flame. Use mesquite alone or with charcoal briquettes. Or, if you wish, merely sprinkle a few pieces of it on top of hot coals to impart flavor. For use with gas grills, follow the directions on the package of mesquite.

Mesquite is available packaged as chunks and as chips. Buy it at specialty food shops and barbecue-equipment vendors. You can also order mesquite by mail; see page 101 for a list of mail-order sources. While by no means essential to the success of a barbecue, mesquite is worth the trouble it takes to track it down. Both Victoria Wise (pages 50–53) and Bruce Cliborne (pages 58–59) call for mesquite to cook their meals.

Gas fuel is available as either piped-in natural gas for permanent installations or as liquid propane stored in tanks at the base of portable grills. The gas heats lava rocks or ceramic briquettes, provided with the grills, to cook the food. Gas grills only take about 10 minutes to heat up, so they are ready to cook more quickly than are other barbecue units. The temperature is also easily adjusted by regulating the gas, so that covered cookers lack the lower air vents necessary for solid fuel units.

Electric grills work in a fashion similar to that of gas models: An electric element heats lava rocks or ceramic briquettes, which are ready to cook on after about 10 minutes. The temperature of the grill is easily adjusted by a knob controlling the electric element.

Firestarters

Jelly, liquid, and wax are safe to use for both wood and charcoal provided you never add them to an already lighted fire. Allow them to soak into the fuel for a couple of minutes before lighting the fire. If your fire is slow, fan it to get it going (but be careful not to spread sparks). Any residual odor from these starters will burn away once the coals are glowing.

None of these products is needed if you use a chimney starter. Chimney starters light charcoal fires swiftly, efficiently, and safely. Place crumpled newspaper in the bottom of the chimney, pile charcoal on top, and light the newspaper through the bottom vent. When the charcoal is burning well, carefully lift the chimney to empty the fuel into the grill. Chimney starters are available at hardware stores, or you may make your own using a large can.

Another firestarting alternative is to use an electric starter. These are plug-in elements that are inserted into stacked charcoal briquettes. They light fuel quickly and

safely, but you must remove the element after eight minutes to prevent burning out the starter. Handle the element carefully after removing it. To start gas or electric grills, follow the manufacturer's instructions.

Building the Fire

The kind of fire you build directly effects the quality of your barbecue. Each fire reacts differently to wind, air temperature, humidity, and how you stack the fuel. The unit you use and the quantity of food you plan to grill determine the amount of fuel you need. For instance, an open brazier needs more fuel than a hooded or covered grill.

To begin, line the bottom of the unit with a layer of heavy-duty aluminum foil. This acts as a heat reflector and makes it easier to clean the grill. If using wood, first crumple sheets of newspaper. Then, stack kindling and split wood around the paper, and heavier wood against the kindling to make a tepee or pyramid shape. Use enough wood to provide a single layer of coals that extends two inches beyond the food.

For wood fire, stack kindling and split wood around crumpled sheets of newspaper.

If using charcoal briquettes, you should have enough to extend two inches beyond the food when you spread them into a single layer. You may reuse the unburned portion for the next barbecue. Unless you are using a chimney, stack the charcoal into a pyramid and ignite it.

For charcoal fire, stack briquettes into a pyramid.

Most fuel takes about half an hour to be ready for cooking. Wood will be ready when the fire has died down to glowing gray coals. Briquettes will be covered with an even gray ash, and are not ready if any black portion is visible. During the day, the coals will appear gray, and at night, red and glowing, with a coating of gray ash. You should see heat waves rising from the grill, which should be hot enough to make food sizzle as soon as it touches the grill. If you are not sure the fire is ready, another way to judge it is to carefully hold your hand, palm down, over the coals four inches above the fire. If you can hold your hand over the coals for only 1 to 2 seconds, your fire is very hot, suitable for steaks; if for 3 to 4 seconds, your fire is medium hot, suitable for poultry; if for 5 seconds, your fire is slow, suitable for large roasts. When the fire is ready, spread the coals into a single layer with long-handled tongs before you start to cook. During cooking, watch the coals—when the gray ash covering them becomes too thick, it will reduce the amount of available heat. Knock off the accumulating ash to maintain a steady temperature. For a wood fire, add more wood as you cook to maintain the temperature.

To adjust the temperature, use a barbecue rake to gather the coals together for a hotter fire and to spread them out for a slower fire. If your unit has an adjustable grill, you can raise or lower it to regulate the speed at which food cooks.

When you have finished cooking, extinguish the fire and dispose of the coals. With covered cookers, put the dome lid on and close all vents. For open braziers, douse the live coals with water. If you wish to save any partially used briquettes, extinguish the fire with a bucket of sand. Before discarding the coals, make sure they are quite cool. If you have lined the barbecue with foil before cooking, you can dispose of the coals easily by picking up the ends of the foil and wrapping the coals into a package. Put this package into a trash container.

BARBECUING TECHNIQUES
Before barbecuing, bring all food to room temperature (60° F) to assure even cooking throughout. Brush the grill with vegetable oil before you put the food on; this prevents food from sticking and makes the grill easier to clean. For extra flavor, scatter fresh or dried herbs, or hickory chips, over the coals as you cook. Victoria Wise (pages 50–51) lays stalks of fresh fennel under the food before cooking. To enhance both flavor and texture, you may also wish to marinate or baste food. Marinades are aromatic sauces in which meats soak prior to cooking. All marinades need to contain oil to lubricate the meat and lemon juice, vinegar, or alcohol, such as beer or wine, to tenderize it. Ideally, the marinade acts as a baste, too. Basting adds flavor to grilled foods and seals in juices. For the best results, brush on the sauce during the last 15 minutes of cooking— this way you taste the sauce and the meat separately. Last-minute basting is particularly important if you use a sugar- or tomato-based sauce. These burn off quickly, long before the meat is cooked.

There are two basic barbecuing techniques: direct and indirect. With the direct method, used with uncovered barbecues, food grills above the hot coals. This method is suitable for fast-cooking foods, such as hamburgers, poultry pieces, shish kebabs, chops, and fish. As with broiling, the food sears, then cooks quickly.

With the indirect method, food cooks by reflected heat in a hooded or covered unit. When cooking indirectly, you may wish to arrange the hot coals around the perimeter of a drip pan. You use the indirect method to cook large roasts, such as Victoria Wise's pork loin (page 55).

For indirect cooking, construct a drip pan:

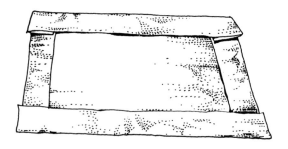

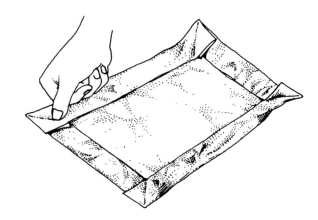

To prevent flare-ups during cooking, which scorch meat and give it a burned taste, remove most excess fat before putting the meat on the grill. Cook by the indirect method if your meat is heavily marbled or you are using a sweet marinade. Or, alternatively, spread lettuce leaves (use the outer leaves of a fresh head of iceberg lettuce) over the hot coals before cooking to prevent fat or a marinade from dripping onto the coals. The lettuce will blacken, but it does not catch on fire. For how to barbecue the foods in this volume, consult the list below.

Beef: Cook steaks and hamburgers over a very hot fire (you may cook larger cuts and roasts over a slower fire). Before barbecuing a steak, score through the fat on the outside, taking care not to cut into the meat. This prevents the meat from curling up. Turn a steak only once, using tongs, taking care not to pierce it. For tender hamburgers, use coarsely ground beef, handle it gently, and form it into firm patties.

Making Chicken Stock

Although canned chicken broth or stock is all right for emergencies, homemade chicken stock has a rich flavor that is hard to match. Moreover, the commercial broths—particularly the canned ones—are likely to be oversalted.

To make your own stock, save chicken parts as they accumulate and put them in a bag in the freezer; then have a rainy-day stock-making session, using one of the recipes here. The skin from a yellow onion will add color; the optional veal bone will add extra flavor and richness to the stock.

Basic Chicken Stock

3 pounds bony chicken parts, such as wings, back, and neck
1 veal knuckle (optional)
3 quarts cold water
1 yellow unpeeled onion, stuck with 2 cloves
2 stalks celery with leaves, cut in two
12 crushed peppercorns
2 carrots, scraped and cut into 2-inch lengths
4 sprigs parsley
1 bay leaf
1 tablespoon fresh thyme, or 1 teaspoon dried
Salt (optional)

1. Wash chicken parts and veal knuckle (if you are using it) and drain. Place in large soup kettle or stockpot (any big pot) with the remaining ingredients—except salt. Cover pot and bring to a boil over medium heat.

2. Lower heat and simmer stock, partly covered, 2 to 3 hours. Skim foam and scum from top of stock several times. Add salt to taste after stock has cooked 1 hour.

3. Strain stock through fine sieve placed over large bowl. Discard chicken pieces, vegetables, and seasonings. Let stock cool uncovered (this will speed cooling process). When completely cool, refrigerate. Fat will rise and congeal conveniently at top. You may skim it off and discard it or leave it as protective covering for stock.

Yield: About 10 cups.

The flavor of chicken stock comes from the bones (as well as the seasonings and vegetables) rather than the meat. The longer you cook the bones, the better the stock. If you would like to poach a whole chicken and want to make a good, strong stock at the same time, this highly economical recipe will accomplish both aims at once.

Strong Chicken Stock

10 cups homemade chicken stock (yield of recipe at left)
1 bay leaf
1 stalk celery
1 carrot, scraped
1 yellow onion, unpeeled
1 whole broiler or fryer (about 3 pounds)

1. Add stock, bay leaf, and vegetables to kettle large enough to hold them and chicken. Bring to a boil over medium heat.

2. Add chicken, breast up, and allow liquid to return to a simmer. Reduce heat and poach chicken with lid slightly ajar.

3. After 40 minutes, test for doneness. Insert long-handled spoon into chicken cavity and remove chicken to platter.

4. When chicken is cool enough to handle, but still warm, debone it, reserving meat for salads or sandwiches but returning skin and bones to cooking pot. Continue to simmer, uncovered, until stock has reduced by half. Proceed as in step 3 of basic stock recipe, left.

Added Touch: If you have time and want a particularly rich-looking stock, put the chicken bones in a shallow baking pan and brown them under the broiler for 10 minutes before you add them to the stock.

Stock freezes well and will keep for three months in the freezer. Use small containers for convenience and freeze in pre-measured amounts: a cup, or half a cup. Or pour the cooled stock into ice cube trays, then remove the frozen cubes and store in a plastic bag. You can drop these frozen cubes directly into your saucepan.

Poultry and rabbit: Cook delicate meats, such as these, over a medium-hot fire. Start pieces of poultry by placing the cut side toward the fire, or skin side upward, to seal in the juices. Turn the pieces as directed in the recipe to keep the skin from blistering and to retain the juices. Use tongs for turning and be careful not to pierce the meat.

Pork: Cook pork over a medium-hot to low fire. Because pork needs to be cooked thoroughly, its cooking time will be longer than for other meat. Grill pork until its juices run clear or, for a pork roast, until its internal temperature is 170° F.

Lamb: Cook lamb roasts over a medium-hot fire; grill chops over a hot fire.

Fish: Cook fish over a medium-hot fire. When grilling large pieces of fish, such as bluefish (pages 43–44), preferably leave the skin intact. This retains moisture and keeps the flesh from falling apart. Before putting the fish on the grill, make several shallow slashes in the skin to keep it from puckering. A hinged metal basket is an excellent tool for barbecuing fish. To keep the fish from sticking, you should oil the skin and the basket, and be sure the grill is completely clean. You may also grill fish wrapped in heavy-duty aluminum foil.

Skewered foods: Cook food on skewers at the same temperature given for that type of food, i.e., a very hot fire for beef, a medium-hot fire for pork, and so on. Cut meat or fish into 1- to 1½-inch cubes and thread them onto the skewer, alternating with vegetable pieces, if desired.

Foil-wrapped vegetables: Cooking temperatures vary with the type of vegetable; follow the instructions given in the individual recipes. Wrap the vegetables in foil, following the instructions on page 9. This is how Nicholas Baxter cooks his Mélange of Fresh Vegetables (page 71).

BASIC COOKING TECHNIQUES

Whether you plan to cook indoors or out, you will probably use one or a combination of several of the following basic cooking methods.

Barbecue Tools

Accessories for outdoor cooking simplify work and reduce the risk of burns. Some basic barbecue tools may already be in your kitchen: a long-handled basting brush, a long-handled spatula, a long-handled fork, tongs, a roasting pan, ovenproof mitts, long fireplace matches, and heavy-duty aluminum foil (for wrapping foods and lining the barbecue). You will also need a small work surface near the grill.

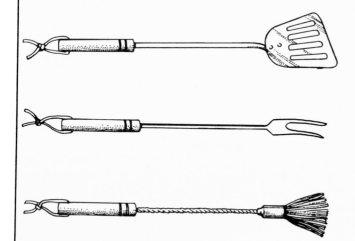

Skewers: These are essential for preparing shish kebabs or any foods cooked *en brochette.* Select flattened skewers so the food stays put during cooking. You need skewers for John Risser's Barbecued Beef Kabobs (page 87).

Hinged grill basket: These two-piece wire-mesh cages adjust to accommodate foods of varying thickness. Several types

of basket are available, and some have long handles for safe and easy turning during cooking. They are particularly useful for barbecuing fish. See Ron Davis's Grilled Bluefish with Spinach, Bread, and Vegetable Stuffing (pages 43–44).

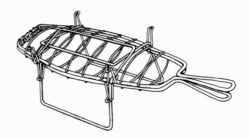

Drip pan: Use a small foil baking pan to catch fat under the grilling meat and help prevent flare-ups. Arrange the coals around the edge of the drip pan.

Instant-reading meat thermometer: To provide an accurate test for doneness, an instant-reading meat thermometer is useful for cooking roasts, such as Victoria Wise's Pork Loin Roasted with Garlic and Sage (page 55).

Flameproof, heatproof mitts: These are essential to protect hands from burns.

Water sprayer or plant mister: This should be kept handy to control or douse flare-ups, especially when you cook very fatty meat or food marinated in sugary marinades. Use the sprayer judiciously: If you soak the fuel you will steam the food, not broil it. To prevent the food from being covered with ash, take it off the grill before spraying, or raise the grill and spray under it.

Sautéing

Sautéing is a form of quick frying, with no cover on the pan. In French, *sauter* means "to jump," which is what vegetables or small pieces of food do when you shake the sauté pan. The purpose is to lightly brown the food and seal in the juices, sometimes before further cooking. This technique has three critical elements: the right pan, the proper temperature, and dry food.

The sauté pan: A proper sauté pan is 10 to 12 inches in diameter and has 2- to 3-inch straight sides that allow you to turn food pieces and still keep the fat from spattering. It has a heavy bottom that slides easily over a burner.

The best material (and the most expensive) for a sauté pan is tin-lined copper because it is a superior heat conductor. Heavy-gauge aluminum works well but will discolor acidic food like tomatoes. Therefore, you should not use aluminum if the food is to be cooked for more than twenty minutes after the initial browning. Another option is to

select a heavy-duty sauté pan made of strong, heat-conductive aluminum alloys. This type of professional cookware is smooth and stick-resistant.

Select a sauté pan large enough to hold the pieces of food without crowding. The heat of the fat and the air spaces around and between the pieces facilitate browning. Crowding results in steaming—a technique that lets the juices out rather than sealing them in. If your sauté pan is not large enough to prevent crowding, separate the food into two batches, or use two pans at once.

Be sure you buy a sauté pan with a tight-fitting cover. Many recipes call for sautéing first, then lowering the heat and cooking the food, covered, for an additional 10 to 20 minutes. Make certain the handle is long and is comfortable to hold.

Never immerse the hot pan in cold water because this will warp the metal. Allow the pan to cool slightly, then add water and let it sit until you are ready to wash it. Use a wooden spatula or tongs to keep food pieces moving in the pan as you shake it over the burner. If the food sticks, as it occasionally will, a metal spatula will loosen it best. Turn the pieces so that all surfaces come into contact with the hot fat and none of them sticks. Do not use a fork when sautéing meat; piercing the meat will toughen it.

The fat: A combination of half butter and half vegetable oil or peanut oil is perfect for most sautéing: it heats to high temperatures without burning and allows you to have a rich butter flavor at the same time. Always use unsalted butter for cooking, since it tastes better and does not add unwanted salt to your recipe.

Butter alone makes a superb tasting sauté, but butter, whether salted or unsalted, burns at a high temperature. If you prefer an all-butter flavor, clarify the butter before you begin. This means removing the milky residue, which is the part that scorches. To clarify butter, heat it in a small saucepan over medium heat and, using a cooking spoon, skim off the foam as it rises to the top and discard it. Keep skimming until no more foam appears. Pour off the remaining oil, making sure to leave the milky residue at the bottom of the pan. The oil is clarified butter; use this for sautés. Ideally, you should clarify butter as you need it. But it is a simple matter to make a large quantity of it and store it in your refrigerator; it will keep for two to three weeks. Some sautéing recipes in this book call for olive oil, which imparts a delicious and distinctive flavor of its own and is less sensitive than butter to high heat. Nevertheless, even the finest olive oil has some residue of fruit pulp, which will scorch over high heat. Watch carefully when you sauté in olive oil; discard any scorched oil and start with fresh if necessary.

To sauté properly, heat the sauté fat until it is hot but not smoking. When you see small bubbles on top of the fat, it is almost hot enough to smoke. In that case, lower the heat. When using unclarified butter and oil together, add the butter to the hot oil. After the foam from the melting butter subsides, you are ready to sauté. If the temperature is just right, the food will sizzle when you slide it into the pan.

Poaching

You poach meat, fish, or chicken, even fruit, exactly as you would an egg, in very hot liquid in a shallow pan on top of the stove. You can use water, or better still, beef, chicken, or fish stock, or a combination of stock and white wine, or even cream. Bring the liquid to the simmering point and add the food. Be prepared to lower the heat if the liquid begins to boil. Lengthy boiling toughens meat and dries it out.

Stir Frying

This is the basic cooking method for Chinese cuisine. This fast-cook method requires very little oil, and the foods—which you stir continuously—fry quickly over a very high heat. This is ideal for cooking bite-size shredded or thinly sliced portions of vegetables, fish, meat or poultry alone or in combination. Jane Uetz (page 25), uses this cooking method for her Stir-Fried Zucchini and Yellow Squash.

Braising

Braised vegetables, cooked in butter or oil and minimal liquid in a covered pot, emerge moist and lightly browned. Root vegetables and leafy greens are particularly suited to this slow-cook method. The cooking liquid for highly seasoned vegetables is usually stock or water. Strong-tasting vegetables like brussels sprouts, fennel, celeriac, and turnips benefit from parboiling first. If you wish, you may brown vegetables before braising: this seals in flavor that otherwise would be lost in the cooking liquid. Sugar added to the braising liuqid offsets the acid taste of vegetables such as tomatoes. You can braise vegetables singly or in combination with others for a blending of flavors.

Roasting and Baking

Originally *roasting* was the term for cooking meat on a revolving spit over an open fire, but now it means cooking meat or poultry in an oven by a dry heat process. Roasting is especially suitable for thick cuts of meat and whole poultry. During the roasting process, you should baste meats several times with the drippings that collect in the pan.

Baking also means cooking food in the oven, but it is a much more versatile technique. You use it for preparing breads, like Victoria Fahey's Picnic Bread (pages 96–97), for cooking a soufflé, or for salt baking, that is, burying meat, fish, or poultry in coarse salt.

Pan Grilling

Sometimes referred to as pan broiling, this technique is similar to sautéing. Food cooks in a small amount of fat, which has been preheated in a heavy skillet or a ridged cast-iron pan. Pan frying is a quick method that retains juices—it is suitable for thin-cut chops, steaks, and other foods that might dry out under a broiler, see Bruce Cliborne's recipe for Grilled Pork Loin with Fresh Thyme (page 62).

Blanching

Blanching, also called parboiling, is an invaluable technique. Immerse whole or cut vegetables for a few moments in boiling water, then "refresh" them—that is, plunge them into cold water to stop their cooking and set their colors. Blanching softens or tenderizes dense or crisp vegetables, often as a preliminary to further cooking by another method, such as stir frying.

WHAT TO DRINK

Picnics and outdoor meals are as varied as are Americans themselves, and the appropriate beverages cover a wide range. What do you drink with barbecue and picnic food? Just about anything from the costliest Champagne down through less expensive sparkling wines, still wines, beers and ales, to soft drinks and iced tea and coffee. Let the food, the weather, the group, and your own tastes dictate. The suggestions with the menus that follow are intended to help you pick a still wine *if you want one*. In almost every case a sparkling wine or good beer, iced tea or a not-very-sweet fresh lemonade would be fine.

Pantry (for this volume)

A well-stocked, properly organized pantry is essential for preparing great meals in the shortest time possible. Whether your pantry consists of a small refrigerator and two or three shelves over the sink, or a large freezer, refrigerator, and entire room just off the kitchen, you must protect staples from heat and light.

In maintaining your pantry, follow these rules:

1. Store staples by kind and date. Canned goods, canisters, and spices need a separate shelf, or a separate spot on a shelf. Date all staples—shelved, refrigerated, or frozen—by writing the date directly on the package or on a bit of masking tape. Then put the oldest ones in front to be sure you use them first.

2. Store flour, sugar, and other dry ingredients in canisters or jars with tight lids. Glass and clear plastic allow you to see at a glance how much remains.

3. Keep a running grocery list so that you can note when a staple is half gone, and be sure to stock up.

ON THE SHELF:

Anchovies
Anchovy fillets, both flat and rolled, come oil-packed, in tins. If you buy whole, salt-packed anchovies, they must be cleaned under running water, skinned, and boned. To bone, separate the fish with your fingers and slip out the backbone.

Baking powder
Baking soda
Capers
Capers are usually packed in vinegar and less frequently in salt. If you use the latter, you should rinse them under cold water before using them.

Dried fruits
apricots
raisins, dark and golden

Flour
all-purpose, bleached or unbleached
cornmeal
May be yellow or white and of various degrees of coarseness. The stone-ground variety, milled to retain the germ of the corn, generally has a superior flavor.

Garlic
Store in a cool, dry, well-ventilated place. Garlic powder and garlic salt are not adequate substitutes for fresh garlic.

Herbs and spices
The flavor of fresh herbs is much better than that of dried. Fresh herbs should be refrigerated and used as soon as possible. The following herbs are perfectly acceptable dried, but buy in small amounts, store airtight in dry area away from heat and light, and use as quickly as possible. In measuring herbs, remember that one part dried will equal three parts fresh. *Note:* Dried chives and parsley should not be on your shelf, since they have little or no flavor; frozen chives are acceptable. Buy whole spices rather than ground, as they keep their flavor much longer. Grind spices at home and store as directed for herbs.

arrowroot
basil
bay leaves
caraway seeds
Cayenne pepper
chervil
chili peppers, whole and ground
chives
cinnamon, sticks and ground
cloves, whole and ground
coriander (cilantro)
coriander seeds
cumin
curry powder, preferably imported
dill
fennel seeds
marjoram
mint
mustard seeds and powdered
nutmeg, whole and ground
oregano
paprika
pepper
black peppercorns
These are unripe peppercorns dried in their husks. Grind with a pepper mill.
green peppercorns
These undried peppercorns come packed in water or vinegar, or freeze-dried.
white peppercorns
These are the same as the black variety, but are picked ripe and husked. Use them in pale sauces when black pepper specks would spoil the appearance.
poppy seeds
red pepper flakes (also called crushed red pepper)
rosemary
saffron
Made from the dried stigmas of a species of crocus, this spice—the most costly of all seasonings—adds both color and flavor.
sage
salt
Use coarse salt—commonly available as Kosher or sea—for its superior flavor, texture, and purity. Kosher salt and sea salt are less salty than table salt. Substitute in the following proportions: three quarters teaspoon table salt equals just under one teaspoon Kosher or sea salt.
sesame seeds
star anise
Star anise, like Western anise, is licorice flavored but is stronger. The pod is brown and star-shaped, with eight points. Use it whole as a garnish, or break it up for greater flavor, as the recipe directs.
tarragon
thyme
turmeric

Honey
Hot pepper sauce
Maple syrup
Nuts, whole, chopped or slivered
almonds
pecans
walnuts

Oils
corn, safflower, or vegetable
Because these neutral-tasting oils have high smoking points, they are good for high-heat sautéing.
olive oil
Sample French, Greek, Spanish, and Italian oils. Olive oil ranges in color from pale yellow to dark green and in taste from mild and delicate to rich and fruity. Different olive oils can be used for different purposes: for example, lighter ones for cooking, stronger ones for salads. The finest quality olive oil is labeled extra-virgin or virgin.
sesame oil
Chinese and Japanese oil
Sold in the Oriental section of most supermarkets, it is almost always used for sea-

soning. Keeps indefinitely when refrigerated.

cold-pressed oil
Lighter and less strongly flavored than Oriental sesame oil, it is used for cooking and for salads.

walnut oil
Rich and nutty tasting. It turns rancid easily, so keep it tightly closed in the refrigerator.

Olives
Greek or oil-cured olives

Onions
Store all dry-skinned onions in a cool, dry, well-ventilated place.

Bermuda onions
Large and mild, with a flattish shape, they are best baked whole or eaten raw, although they can be used in cooking. They are generally yellow but also may be red or white.

red or Italian onions
Zesty tasting and generally eaten raw. The perfect salad onion.

Spanish onions
Very large with a sweet flavor, they are best for stuffing and baking and are also eaten raw. Perfect for sandwiches.

shallots
The most subtle member of the onion family, the shallot has a delicate garlic flavor.

yellow onions
All-purpose cooking onions, strong in taste.

white onions
Also called boiling onions, these small onions are almost always cooked and served whole.

Pasta and noodles
orzo
shells
spirals

Potatoes, boiling and baking
"New" potatoes are not a particular kind of potato, but any potato that has not been stored.

Rice
long-grain white rice
Slender grains, much

longer than they are wide, that become light and fluffy when cooked and are best for general use.

Soy sauce
Stock, chicken
For maximum flavor and quality, your own stock is best (see recipes page 13), but canned stock, or broth, is adequate for most recipes and convenient to have on hand.

Sugar
dark brown sugar
light brown sugar
confectioners' sugar
granulated sugar

Tomatoes
Italian plum tomatoes
Canned plum tomatoes (preferably imported) are an acceptable substitute for fresh.

tomato paste
Also for sauces. Spoon single tablespoons of unused canned paste onto wax paper and freeze them. Lift frozen paste off and store in plastic container. Sometimes available in tubes, which can be stored in the refrigerator after a small amount is used.

Vinegars
apple cider vinegar (also called cider vinegar)
Use for a mild, fruity flavor.
balsamic vinegar
Aged vinegar with a complex sweet and sour taste
red and white wine vinegars
sherry vinegar
Somewhat less sharp than most wine vinegars, it has a deeper, fuller flavor.
tarragon vinegar
A white wine vinegar flavored with fresh tarragon, it is especially good in salads.

Water chestnuts, canned
Fresh in flavor and crunchy in texture, they are the bulbs of an Asian marsh plant, not chestnuts at all.

Wines and spirits
sherry, sweet and dry
red wine, dry

vermouth, sweet and dry
white wine, dry
Worcestershire sauce

IN THE REFRIGERATOR:

Bread crumbs
You need never buy bread crumbs. To make fresh crumbs, use fresh or day-old bread and process in food processor or blender. For dried, toast bread 30 minutes in preheated 250-degree oven, turning occasionally to prevent slices from browning. Proceed as for fresh. Store bread crumbs in an airtight container: fresh crumbs in the refrigerator, and dried crumbs in a cool, dry place. Either type may also be frozen for several weeks if tightly wrapped in a plastic bag.

Butter
Many cooks prefer unsalted butter because of its finer flavor and because it does not burn as easily as salted.

Cheese
Cheddar cheese, sharp
A firm cheese, ranging in color from nearly white to yellow. Cheddar is a versatile cooking cheese.

Parmesan cheese
Avoid the preground packaged variety; it is very expensive and almost flavorless. Buy Parmesan by the quarter- or half-pound wedge and grate as needed: 4 ounces produces about one cup of grated cheese. Romano, far less costly, can be substituted, but its flavor is considerably sharper—or try mixing the two.

Pecorino Romano cheese
The hard texture of this sharp-tasting Italian cheese makes it ideal for grating.

Cream
half-and-half
heavy cream
light cream
sour cream

Crème fraîche, homemade or commercial

Eggs
Will keep 4 to 5 weeks in refrigerator. For best results, bring to room temperature before using.

Ginger, fresh
Found in the produce section. Ginger will stay fresh in the refrigerator for approximately 1 week, wrapped in plastic. To preserve it longer, place the whole ginger root in a small sherry-filled jar; it will last almost indefinitely, although not without changes in the ginger. Or, if you prefer, store it in the freezer, where it will last about 3 months. Newly purchased ginger need not be peeled.

Lemons
In addition to its many uses in cooking, a slice of lemon rubbed over cut apples and pears will keep them from discoloring. Do not substitute bottled juice or lemon extract.

Limes
Mayonnaise
Milk
Mustards
The recipes in this book usually call for Dijon or coarse-ground mustard.

Parsley
The two most commonly available kinds of parsley are flat-leaved and curly; they can be used interchangeably when necessary. Flat-leaved parsley has a more distinctive flavor and is generally preferred in cooking. Curly parsley wilts less easily and is excellent for garnishing. Store parsley in a glass of water and cover loosely with a plastic bag. It will keep for a week in the refrigerator. Or wash and dry it, and refrigerate in a small plastic bag with a dry paper towel inside to absorb any moisture.

Scallions
Scallions have a mild onion flavor. Store wrapped in plastic.

Yogurt, plain

Equipment

Proper cooking equipment makes the work light and is a good cook's most prized possession. You can cook expertly without a store-bought steamer or even a food processor, but basic pans, knives, and a few other items are indispensable. Below are the things you need—and some attractive options—for preparing the menus in this volume.

Pots and pans
Large kettle or stockpot
3 skillets (large, medium, small), with covers
2 sauté pans, 10 to 12 inches in diameter, with covers and ovenproof handles
3 saucepans with covers (1-, 2-, and 4-quart capacities)
  Choose enameled cast-iron, plain cast-iron, aluminum-clad stainless steel, and heavy aluminum (but you need at least one saucepan that is not aluminum). Best—but very expensive—is tin-lined copper.
Double boiler
Roasting pan
Broiler pan
13 x 9 x 2-inch baking pan
2 cookie sheets (11 x 17-inch and 15½ x 12-inch)
18-inch jelly-roll pan
8½ x 4¼ x 3-inch loaf pan
2- or 3-quart casserole with cover
Four 6-ounce custard cups
Platters

Knives
A carbon-steel knife takes a sharp edge but tends to rust. You must wash and dry it after each use; otherwise it can blacken foods and counter tops. Good-quality stainless steel knives, frequently honed, are less trouble and will serve just as well in the home kitchen. Never put a fine knife in the dishwasher. Rinse it, dry it, and put it away—but not loose in a drawer. Knives will stay sharp and last a long time if they have their own storage rack.
Small paring knife (sharp-pointed end)
10-inch chef's knife
Sharpening steel

Other cooking tools
2 sets of mixing bowls in graduated sizes
Flour sifter
Colander, with a round base

Strainers (preferably 2, in fine and coarse mesh)
Sieve, coarse and fine mesh
2 sets of measuring cups and spoons in graduated sizes
  One for dry ingredients, another for shortenings and liquids.
Slotted spoon
3 long-handled wooden spoons
Wooden spatula (for stirring hot ingredients)
Metal spatula, or turner (for lifting hot foods from pans)
Slotted spatula
Flexible-blade spatula
Rubber or vinyl spatula (for folding in ingredients)
Grater (metal, with several sizes of holes)
  A rotary grater is handy for hard cheese.
2 wire whisks
Pair of metal tongs
Wooden chopping board
Vegetable steamer
Soup ladle
Nutcracker
4 poultry skewers
Cooling rack
Kitchen scissors
Kitchen timer
Stiff scrubbing brush
Kitchen string
Toothpicks
Aluminum foil
Paper towels
Plastic wrap
Wax paper
Thin rubber gloves

Electric appliances
Food processor or blender
  A blender will do most of the work required in this volume, but a food processor will do it more quickly and in larger volume. A food processor should be considered a necessity, not a luxury, for anyone who enjoys cooking.
Electric mixer

Barbecue tools
Barbecue
Drip pan
Long-handled cooking spoon
Long-handled slotted spoon
Long-handled metal spatula
Long-handled, 2-pronged fork
Long-handled tongs
Long-handled basting brush
Four 8- to 12-inch metal skewers
Hinged grill basket
Instant-reading meat thermometer
Heatproof mitt
Fire rake

Picnic equipment
Thermos®
Ice chest
Packing containers

Optional cooking tools
Large cast-iron grilling pan
Wok
Salad spinner
Carving board
Carving knife
Oyster knife
Apple corer
Chinese wok spatulas
Salad servers
Citrus juicer
  Inexpensive glass kind from the dime store will do.
Melon baller
Kitchen mallet
Rolling pin
Flametamer or asbestos mat
Garlic press
Deep fat thermometer
Zester
Nut grinder
Cake tester
Roll of masking tape or white paper tape for labeling and dating

SHARPENING STEEL

BREAD KNIFE

CHEF'S KNIFE

PARING KNIFE

WHISK

SLOTTED
SPATULA

RUBBER SPATULA

STEAMER

GRATER

CITRUS JUICER

DOUBLE BOILER

SAUCEPANS

METAL TONGS

SLOTTED SPOON

SAUTÉ PAN

STRAINER

Jane Uetz

MENU 1 (Left)
Oriental Chicken and Rice Salad
Chinese Cabbage, Snow Peas, and Cucumber
with Curried Mayonnaise
Pineapple with Orange-Chocolate Sauce

MENU 2
Butterflied Leg of Lamb with Savory Sauce
Stir-Fried Zucchini and Yellow Squash
Fresh Mint and Watercress Salad

MENU 3
Monterey Beef Roast
Roast Potatoes with Herbed Butter
Carrot and Broccoli Salad

When planning her meals, whether formal or informal, Jane Uetz likes to inject a surprise element, a special touch that elicits comments from her guests. This could mean a simple meal with a spectacular dessert or one with an exotic appetizer. An example of her approach is Menu 2 in which she features a grilled butterflied leg of lamb, a sumptuous and distinctive cut of meat that has marinated in a flavorful piquant sauce. In Menu 3, the main course is an unusual beef roast that is coated with mustard and salt, then placed directly onto hot coals for grilling.

Her style of cooking is light, fresh, and uncomplicated. She willingly experiments with flavors and may combine several cuisines in one meal. For the picnic in Menu 1, she offers an Oriental salad consisting of chicken breasts cut into strips and combined with chilled rice, red pepper, and scallions. Although the green salad calls for two Chinese vegetables, she seasons them with an Indian curry-flavored mayonnaise. And her dessert has French overtones—fresh pineapple served with an orange-chocolate sauce.

A wicker basket lined with bandannas contains a picnic in three separate bowls: chicken and rice salad; cabbage, snow-pea, and cucumber salad; and chunks of fresh pineapple with orange-chocolate sauce on the side.

21

Oriental Chicken and Rice Salad
Chinese Cabbage, Snow Peas, and Cucumber with Curried Mayonnaise
Pineapple with Orange-Chocolate Sauce

This picnic consists of two substantial main-course salads, one of meat and one of vegetables, and a refreshing pineapple dessert. The vegetable salad calls for Chinese cabbage, also known as Napa or celery cabbage, a variety with a long head that somewhat resembles Romaine lettuce. Its broad leaves are crinkly and tender, and often fringed with pale green. Chinese cabbage has a fresh, delicate noncabbagey flavor.

Chinese pea pods, or snow peas, are another component of this salad. These edible pods are sweet, crisp, and delicious raw. Select unblemished, firm green pods and refrigerate them in a plastic bag. Sugar snap peas make good substitutes.

Carry the chocolate sauce for the pineapple in a small Thermos® container, or pour it hot into a jar and wrap the jar in a towel.

WHAT TO DRINK

Serve cold beer, light ale, or a fruity, cold white wine. Italian Pinot Grigio or Pinot Bianco would be excellent choices, as would a French Muscadet.

SHOPPING LIST AND STAPLES

2 whole chicken breasts, skinned and boned (about 1 pound total weight)
Small Chinese cabbage (about 2 pounds)
¼ pound snow peas
Small red bell pepper
Small cucumber
Small bunch scallions
½-inch piece fresh ginger
Medium-size pineapple (about 3½ pounds)
1⅔ cup chicken stock, preferably homemade (see page 13), or canned
1 tablespoon unsalted butter
1 tablespoon vegetable oil
¼ cup cold-pressed (not Oriental) sesame seed oil
1 tablespoon white wine vinegar
⅓ cup good-quality commercial mayonnaise
3 tablespoons soy sauce
Hot pepper sauce
¾ cup long-grain rice
¼ cup sugar
2 ounces unsweetened chocolate
6-ounce package semisweet chocolate bits

3-ounce can pecans, unsalted peanuts, or cashews
1 teaspoon curry powder
Salt
2 tablespoons dry sherry
½ cup orange liqueur

UTENSILS

2 medium-size saucepans, one with cover
Double boiler
Salad bowl
Medium-size bowl
2 small bowls
Cutting board
2 platters
Salad spinner (optional)
Colander
Measuring cups and spoons
Chef's knife
Paring knife
Slotted spoon
Wooden spoon
Salad servers
Teaspoon
Whisk
Grater
Vegetable peeler (optional)
Small jar with lid plus additional jar, if not using Thermos®
Thermos®

START-TO-FINISH STEPS

1. Follow chicken salad recipe steps 1 through 3.
2. While chicken is poaching, grate ginger and coarsely chop nuts for salad recipe. Halve cabbage lengthwise and follow cabbage recipe step 1.
3. Follow chicken recipe steps 4 and 5.
4. While chicken and rice are cooling, follow cabbage recipe steps 2 through 4, and pineapple recipe steps 1 and 2.
5. Follow chicken recipe steps 6 through 11 and cabbage recipe step 5.
6. Follow pineapple recipe steps 3 and 4, and pack picnic if transporting.
7. Follow chicken recipe step 12, cabbage recipe step 6, and serve.
8. For dessert, follow pineapple recipe step 5 and serve.

22

Oriental Chicken and Rice Salad

½ teaspoon salt
¾ cup long-grain rice
1⅔ cups chicken stock
2 whole chicken breasts, skinned and boned
  (about 1 pound total weight)
Small red bell pepper
3 scallions
¼ cup cold-pressed sesame seed oil
3 tablespoons soy sauce
2 tablespoons dry sherry
1 teaspoon freshly grated ginger
¼ teaspoon hot pepper sauce
½ cup coarsely chopped pecans, unsalted peanuts,
  or cashews

1. In medium-size saucepan, combine ½ teaspoon salt and 1½ cups water. Cover and bring to a boil over medium-high heat.
2. Add rice to boiling water, stir once with fork, and reduce heat to a gentle simmer. Cover pan and cook exactly 18 minutes.
3. While rice is cooking, bring stock to a boil in another medium-size saucepan over medium-high heat. Add chicken breasts, reduce heat to a gentle simmer, and poach breasts 10 to 15 minutes, or until a knife inserted in the center of the chicken breasts reveals rosy white flesh.
4. With slotted spoon, transfer chicken breasts to cutting board or counter. Let breasts cool slightly, about 15 minutes.
5. Remove rice from heat, fluff lightly with fork, and spread out on platter to cool, about 15 minutes.
6. Wash red pepper and pat dry with paper towels. Core, halve, and seed pepper. Cut into slivers.
7. Wash scallions and pat dry with paper towels. With chef's knife, trim off ends and cut into 1-inch lengths.
8. With chef's knife, cut cooled chicken breasts into ¼-inch strips.
9. In medium-size bowl, combine red pepper, scallions, chicken strips, and cooled rice, and toss gently with fork to combine.
10. In small bowl, combine sesame oil, soy sauce, sherry, ginger, and hot pepper sauce. Pour over salad and toss with fork until evenly coated.
11. Cover salad with plastic wrap and chill until ready to leave for picnic or to serve.
12. Just before serving, add nuts and toss with fork to combine.

Chinese Cabbage, Snow Peas, and Cucumber with Curried Mayonnaise

½ small head Chinese cabbage
¼ pound snow peas
Small cucumber
⅓ cup mayonnaise
1 tablespoon vegetable oil
1 tablespoon white wine vinegar
1 teaspoon curry powder

1. Peel off any damaged outer leaves from cabbage and discard. With chef's knife, cut cabbage crosswise into 1-inch-wide pieces. In colander, wash and drain cabbage. Dry in salad spinner or pat dry with paper towels and transfer to salad bowl.
2. Trim and string snow peas. Wash under cold water and pat dry with paper towels. With chef's knife, cut snow peas lengthwise into ¼-inch julienne strips. Add to salad bowl.
3. With vegetable peeler or paring knife, peel cucumber. Halve cucumber lengthwise and, with teaspoon, scoop out seeds. Lay each half cut side down and cut into ½-inch-thick slices. Add to salad bowl.
4. With salad servers, toss salad ingredients to combine. Cover bowl with plastic wrap, and chill at least 15 minutes or until ready to leave for picnic or to serve.
5. For dressing, combine remaining ingredients in small bowl and whisk until blended. Transfer to small jar with lid and refrigerate until ready to leave for picnic or to serve. If transporting in hot weather, be sure to pack dressing in ice chest.
6. Just before serving, spoon dressing over salad and, with salad servers, toss to coat.

Pineapple with Orange-Chocolate Sauce

Medium-size pineapple (about 3½ pounds)
2 ounces unsweetened chocolate, broken into pieces
½ cup semisweet chocolate bits
1 tablespoon unsalted butter
¼ cup sugar
½ cup orange liqueur

1. With chef's knife, cut ¾-inch-thick slice from top and bottom of pineapple and discard.
2. Pare pineapple, starting from top and following contours of pineapple with knife. With tip of paring knife or vegetable peeler, remove eyes. Cutting from top to bottom, cut pineapple into ½- to ¾-inch-thick slices. Halve each slice crosswise and cut out core. Cut slices into fingers, about ½ to 1 inch wide by 4 inches long. Arrange on platter, cover loosely with plastic wrap, and chill at least 20 minutes or until ready to serve.
3. In top of double boiler, combine unsweetened chocolate, chocolate bits, and butter. In bottom of double boiler, bring about 1 inch of water to a boil. Reduce heat to a simmer and set top of double boiler into bottom. Heat mixture, stirring occasionally, until chocolate melts, about 3 minutes.
4. With whisk, stir mixture until well blended. Still stirring, add sugar and orange liqueur, and cook, stirring constantly, until sauce is thick and smooth and sugar has melted, 4 to 5 minutes. Transfer to Thermos® or to jar. If using jar, wrap immediately in towel to keep warm.
5. Just before serving, stir sauce to recombine, if necessary, and spoon it into small Chinese teacups or other small bowls for dipping.

Butterflied Leg of Lamb with Savory Sauce
Stir-Fried Zucchini and Yellow Squash
Fresh Mint and Watercress Salad

To serve this barbecue, lay out decorative placemats for your diners. Arrange the lamb slices topped with sauce and the stir-fried squash on individual plates and serve the watercress salad separately.

To organize this barbecue properly, prepare the salad while the lamb is grilling. When the lamb is done, let it rest off the fire while you stir fry the zucchini and yellow squash and toss the salad at the very last moment.

To butterfly a leg of lamb means to debone the meat, leaving one large flat piece with a butterfly shape. Unless you are very skilled at carving, ask your butcher to do this. This cut of lamb is delicious barbecued, but because it is not uniformly thick, some portions of the meat will cook more quickly than others.

WHAT TO DRINK

The best accompaniment to this meal is a fruity young Zinfandel or a Beaujolais. A good beer or ale would also be appropriate.

SHOPPING LIST AND STAPLES

4-pound leg of lamb, boned and butterflied
Small zucchini
Small yellow squash
Medium-size onion plus 1 small onion
2 cloves garlic
2 bunches watercress
Small bunch fresh basil, or 1 teaspoon dried
Small bunch fresh mint leaves, or 2 teaspoons dried
6 tablespoons unsalted butter
1 tablespoon safflower oil
2 tablespoons walnut oil
3 tablespoons cider vinegar
1 tablespoon red wine vinegar
1 tablespoon Worcestershire sauce
3 tablespoons catsup
¼ teaspoon Tabasco sauce
2 tablespoons dark brown sugar
1 tablespoon dry mustard
½ teaspoon paprika
1 bay leaf
Salt and freshly ground pepper

UTENSILS

Barbecue
Large skillet
Small saucepan
Salad bowl
Small bowl

Salad spinner (optional)
Colander
Cutting board
Measuring cups and spoons
Chef's knife
Carving knife (optional)
Paring knife
Wooden spoon
Salad servers
Long-handled double-pronged fork

START-TO-FINISH STEPS

Thirty minutes ahead: Start barbecue and bring lamb to room temperature.

1. Follow lamb recipe steps 1 through 3.
2. While lamb is grilling, peel and finely mince onion for lamb and squash recipes.
3. Follow salad recipe steps 1 through 3.
4. Follow lamb recipe steps 4 and 5.
5. While lamb is grilling, wash, dry, and chop fresh basil, if using, and follow squash recipe steps 1 and 2.
6. Follow lamb recipe step 6.
7. While lamb is resting, follow squash recipe steps 3 through 5.
8. Follow salad recipe step 4, lamb recipe step 7, and serve with squash.

RECIPES

Butterflied Leg of Lamb with Savory Sauce

1 clove garlic
4-pound leg of lamb, boned and butterflied, at room
   temperature
Salt and freshly ground pepper
4 tablespoons unsalted butter
3 tablespoons cider vinegar
3 tablespoons catsup
2 tablespoons dark brown sugar
1 tablespoon dry mustard
1 tablespoon Worcestershire sauce
1 tablespoon finely minced onion
1 bay leaf
½ teaspoon paprika
¼ teaspoon hot pepper sauce

1. Peel garlic and cut into slivers.
2. With paring knife, make several ¾- to 1-inch-deep slits in lamb and, with your fingers, insert a garlic sliver in each of the slits. Sprinkle lamb with salt and pepper to taste and pat meat to make seasoning adhere.
3. Place meat on grill, fat side down, 4 to 6 inches from source of heat. Grill 15 minutes for rare and 20 minutes for medium.
4. With long-handled double-pronged fork, turn lamb, and grill 15 to 20 minutes more, or until outside is crusty brown and interior has reached desired degree of doneness.

5. In small saucepan set on burner or side of barbecue grill, melt butter. Add ¼ cup water, 1 teaspoon salt, and remaining ingredients, and stir with fork until blended. Cook mixture, uncovered, stirring occasionally, over medium-low heat 20 minutes.
6. Transfer lamb to cutting board and allow meat to rest 10 minutes before slicing. Cover sauce and keep warm until ready to serve.
7. Cut meat into ½-inch-thick slices and top with warm sauce.

Stir-Fried Zucchini and Yellow Squash

½ clove garlic
Small zucchini
Small yellow squash
2 tablespoons unsalted butter
Medium-size onion, peeled and minced
1 tablespoon chopped fresh basil, or 1 teaspoon dried
Salt and freshly ground pepper

1. Peel and mince garlic.
2. Wash zucchini and yellow squash, and pat dry with paper towels. With chef's knife, cut into ¼-inch-thick slices.
3. In large skillet, melt butter over medium-high heat. Add garlic and onion and, stirring with wooden spoon, stir fry until onion is barely crisp-tender, 2 to 3 minutes.
4. Add zucchini, yellow squash, and basil, and stir fry another 2 to 3 minutes, or until squash is crisp-tender.
5. Remove pan from heat, season with salt and pepper to taste, and stir to blend. Keep mixture warm over very low heat until ready to serve.

Fresh Mint and Watercress Salad

2 bunches watercress
1 cup whole, fresh mint leaves, or 2 teaspoons dried
2 tablespoons walnut oil
1 tablespoon safflower oil
1 tablespoon red wine vinegar
Salt and freshly ground pepper

1. In colander, wash watercress and fresh mint, if using, and dry in salad spinner or pat dry with paper towels. Remove stems and discard.
2. In salad bowl, combine watercress and mint leaves. Cover with plastic wrap and refrigerate until ready to serve.
3. In small bowl, combine walnut and safflower oils, vinegar, dried mint leaves, if not using fresh, and salt and pepper to taste. With fork, beat until blended. Set aside.
4. Just before serving, stir dressing to recombine and pour over salad. With salad servers, toss greens until lightly coated. Divide among individual plates or bowls.

LEFTOVER SUGGESTION

Leftover lamb can be julienned and added to stir-fried vegetables for a simple main dish. Or, it may be sliced and served cold on a vegetable platter with a light vinaigrette.

Monterey Beef Roast
Roast Potatoes with Herbed Butter
Carrot and Broccoli Salad

Garnish the beef roast with watercress sprigs and a lemon twist, if desired, and serve the potatoes in their foil wrapping.

For this barbecue, both the beef roast and the potatoes are grilled simultaneously, so prepare your salad while they are cooking.

The beef roast for this barbecue is a dish Jane Uetz discovered in California many years ago. The beef is covered with mustard, coated completely with a crust of coarse salt, then laid directly on a bed of hot coals. The salt coating will turn black as the meat sears, sealing in the juices.

WHAT TO DRINK

The beef roast calls for a robust red wine. First choice would be a California Zinfandel; second, but equally good, would be a Rhône wine like Châteauneuf-du-Pape.

SHOPPING LIST AND STAPLES

2-to 2½-pound rib eye beef roast
4 medium-size Idaho potatoes
Small bunch broccoli (about 1 pound)
2 large carrots
Small head Boston lettuce
4 tablespoons unsalted butter
2-ounce jar pimentos
3½-ounce jar capers
⅓ cup vegetable oil
2 tablespoons red wine vinegar
½ cup Dijon mustard, approximately
¼ teaspoon paprika
¼ teaspoon dried leaf oregano
¼ teaspoon dried basil
2 cups coarse (kosher) salt
Salt and freshly ground pepper

UTENSILS

Barbecue
Medium-size saucepan with cover
2 platters
Medium-size bowl
2 small bowls
Salad spinner (optional)

Colander
Strainer
Measuring cups and spoons
Chef's knife
Carving knife
Paring knife
Wooden spoon
Slotted spoon
Flexible-blade spatula or butter knife
Instant-reading meat thermometer
Barbecue tongs
Pastry brush

START-TO-FINISH STEPS

Thirty minutes ahead: Start barbecue: Prepare a bed of coals 2 to 3 inches deep.

1. Follow potatoes recipe steps 1 through 3 and roast recipe steps 1 through 3. (To calculate when to start beef roast, subtract desired cooking time plus 10-minute resting time from time at which potatoes will be done.)
2. While beef is cooking, follow salad recipe steps 1 through 12 and potatoes recipe step 4.
3. Follow potatoes recipe step 5 and roast recipe step 4.
4. Follow salad recipe step 13, potatoes recipe step 6, and serve with beef roast.

RECIPES

Monterey Beef Roast

2-to 2½-pound rib eye beef roast
½ cup Dijon mustard, approximately
2 cups coarse (kosher) salt, approximately

1. Using flexible-blade spatula or butter knife, spread meat evenly with a thick coat of mustard.
2. Pat on as much salt as will cling to the mustard.
3. When coals are covered with gray ash, gently place roast directly on top of them. Using tongs, give meat quarter turn every 10 minutes, always setting it down on top of fresh coals. Cook 25 to 30 minutes for rare (internal temperature of 140 degrees), 30 to 35 minutes for medium-rare (160 degrees), and 35 to 40 minutes for well done (170 degrees).
4. Transfer beef to platter and let rest 10 minutes.

Roast Potatoes with Herbed Butter

4 tablespoons unsalted butter
4 medium-size Idaho potatoes
¼ teaspoon paprika
¼ teaspoon dried leaf oregano
¼ teaspoon dried basil, crumbled
¼ teaspoon salt
Pinch of freshly ground pepper

1. Place butter in small bowl and allow to come to room temperature.
2. Scrub potatoes, rinse, and pat dry with paper towels.

Cut potatoes crosswise into ¼-inch-thick slices without cutting through potato. Slices must stay attached.
3. Cut four 8 x 8-inch sheets of aluminum foil. Place each potato in center of sheet, roll up edges, and crimp to seal. Place potatoes directly on hot coals and bake 40 minutes, turning several times during baking.
4. Add remaining ingredients to butter and stir to blend.
5. With tongs, transfer potatoes to platter. Open foil wrapping. With pastry brush, brush each potato with butter mixture, coating inside surfaces of each slice. Re-wrap loosely and return potatoes to coals. Bake another 10 to 15 minutes, or until flesh yields easily when pressed.
6. With tongs, transfer potatoes to platter with beef, peel back foil, and serve.

Carrot and Broccoli Salad

Small bunch broccoli (about 1 pound)
2 large carrots
2-ounce jar pimentos
3½-ounce jar capers
⅓ cup vegetable oil
2 tablespoons red wine vinegar
¼ teaspoon salt
⅛ teaspoon pepper
Small head Boston lettuce

1. Wash broccoli and cut into bite-size florets.
2. Scrape carrots, trim off ends, and cut on diagonal into ¼-inch-thick slices.
3. In medium-size saucepan, bring 1 inch of water to a boil over medium-high heat.
4. Add broccoli florets to boiling water, cover, and cook 1 minute, or until florets are crisp-tender.
5. With slotted spoon, transfer florets to colander, reserving cooking water, and refresh under cold running water 1 to 2 minutes. Keep water in pan boiling.
6. Add carrots to boiling water, cover, and cook 2 to 3 minutes, or until crisp-tender.
7. Add carrots to broccoli and refresh under cold running water 1 to 2 minutes.
8. Drain broccoli and carrots and turn into medium-size bowl.
9. In strainer, drain pimentos and chop enough to measure 2 tablespoons. Reserve remainder for other use.
10. In strainer, drain capers and, if salt-packed, rinse thoroughly under cold running water. Chop enough capers to measure 2 teaspoons.
11. For dressing, combine oil, vinegar, pimentos, capers, salt, and pepper in small bowl and beat with fork. Pour dressing over vegetables and toss until vegetables are evenly coated. Cover with plastic wrap and refrigerate until ready to serve.
12. Wash lettuce and dry in salad spinner or pat dry with paper towels. Line serving platter with lettuce, cover with plastic wrap, and refrigerate until needed.
13. Remove vegetables and platter from refrigerator. With wooden spoon, toss vegetables to recombine with dressing and spoon mixture onto lettuce-lined platter.

Roberta Rall

MENU 1 (Right)
Grilled Cornish Hens with Oriental Flavors
Stir-Fried Carrots with Snow Peas
Fresh Fruit in Cookie Cups

MENU 2
Grilled Monkfish with Lime-Butter Baste
Marinated Vegetables
Bulgur with Carrots and Scallions

MENU 3
Great Grilled Burgers
Raw Vegetables with Creamy Basil Dip
Fruit Layers with Vanilla Sauce

Home economist Roberta Rall keeps three questions in mind when she develops her recipes. First, does the recipe use time and ingredients economically? Menu 1 is an example of this practical approach. The marinade for the Cornish game hens is used as the cooking liquid for the stir-fried vegetables and, subsequently, it is served as a dunking sauce for the cooked hens.

Second, are all the ingredients readily available? She suggests three choices of seafood for the entrée of Menu 2. Use either monkfish, shrimp, or catfish—depending on what is fresh in your marketplace. They are all firm-fleshed and therefore can be cooked on skewers without falling apart. If coriander, also known as Chinese parsley, is unavailable, use regular parsley instead. Substitutes will have a different flavor but will be just as delicious.

Third, can an inexperienced cook recreate the recipe? In Menu 3, she works with a basic dish that most home cooks know—hamburgers. To make these barbecued hamburgers special, she dresses them up with several variations: grated cheese, chopped avocado, sour cream, lettuce, and tomatoes or sautéed onions and mushrooms. Cooks can personalize the other components of the meal, too: For the raw vegetable platter and the fruit compote, select whatever seasonal produce suits your taste.

When you serve this barbecue, set one tray per guest, offering each a grilled game hen garnished with watercress and a portion of the stir-fried carrots, snow peas and water chestnuts. The baked cookie cups are filled with blueberries and raspberries.

Grilled Cornish Hens with Oriental Flavors
Stir-Fried Carrots with Snow Peas
Fresh Fruit in Cookie Cups

Marinated Rock Cornish game hens, served hot from the barbecue grill, are the focal point of this meal. Bake the cookie cups first, then fill them with fruit just before serving.

Rock Cornish game hens are a cross between two different chickens: the Cornish, an English strain, and an American White Plymouth Rock. Allow one bird per serving. They usually come frozen but are occasionally available fresh. Game hens have mild-flavored white meat needing extra seasoning. For this recipe, the hens soak in a flavorful soy-based marinade that calls for Oriental sesame oil, an amber-colored oil with an intense nutty flavor.

To stir fry the carrots, snow peas, and water chestnuts, use a wok, the traditional Chinese pan used for quick-cooking foods. Woks usually come with a lid, which allows you to steam, as you do with the carrots in this recipe. Because they are firm, carrots require extra cooking before you add the water chestnuts and delicate snow peas. When all the vegetables are combined, stir them constantly with a Chinese metal wok spatula or long-handled spoons to keep them from scorching. If you have no wok, use a heavy-gauge sauté pan.

The cookie cups are an adaptation of the classic French *tuiles*—cookies shaped like the curved tiles on old French farmhouses. For this version, you push the baked, but still soft, cookies into custard cups, and the dough cools and hardens into an edible petal-shaped container for the fruit. If you wish, make the cookies ahead and store them in an airtight container. Because moisture from the fruit may cause the cookie bottoms to soften, fill the cookies just before serving.

WHAT TO DRINK

The flavors of this menu are somewhat spicy as well as slightly sweet, so your wine choice can accentuate either flavor. For a bit of sweetness, opt for a Riesling; for spiciness, choose a Gewürztraminer.

SHOPPING LIST AND STAPLES

4 Rock Cornish hens (about 1½ pounds each)
3 carrots (about ¼ pound total weight)
½ pound snow peas
4 cloves garlic
3-inch piece fresh ginger
Small bunch watercress (optional)
2 pints summer berries (blueberries or raspberries), or 3 cups cut-up fresh fruit of your choice (kiwis, grapes, orange sections, bananas, or papayas), or 1 pint vanilla ice cream
1 orange (optional)
1 egg
2 tablespoons milk
4 tablespoons unsalted butter
8-ounce can water chestnuts
3 tablespoons peanut oil
1 tablespoon Oriental sesame oil
¾ cup soy sauce
½ cup confectioners' sugar
¼ cup all-purpose flour
4-ounce can walnut pieces

UTENSILS

Barbecue
Food processor (optional)
Wok or large heavy-gauge skillet with cover
Small saucepan
13 x 9 x 2-inch baking dish
Two 17 x 11-inch baking sheets
Wire rack
Four 6-ounce custard cups
Medium-size bowl
Measuring cups and spoons
Chef's knife
Paring knife
Wooden spoon
Metal spatula
Chinese metal wok spatula or 2 wooden spoons
Barbecue tongs
Whisk (if not using electric mixer)
Vegetable peeler
Electric mixer or whisk
Grater
Nut grinder (if not using processor)
Poultry or kitchen shears
Kitchen mallet
Basting brush

START-TO-FINISH STEPS

1. Start barbecue.
2. Follow Cornish hens recipe steps 1 through 3.

3. While hens are marinating, grind walnuts, grate orange peel, if using, and follow cookie cups recipe steps 1 through 6.

4. While cookies are baking, prepare fruit, if using, and refrigerate until ready to serve.

5. Follow Cornish hens recipe step 4.

6. While hens are grilling, follow carrots recipe steps 1 through 3.

7. If using watercress as garnish for hens, wash and pat dry.

8. Five minutes before Cornish hens are done, follow recipe step 5 and carrots recipe steps 4 and 5.

9. Follow Cornish hens recipe step 6 and serve with carrots.

10. For dessert, follow cookie cups recipe step 7 and serve.

RECIPES

Grilled Cornish Hens with Oriental Flavors

4 Rock Cornish hens (about 1½ pounds each)
4 cloves garlic
3-inch piece fresh ginger
¾ cup soy sauce
3 tablespoons peanut oil
1 tablespoon Oriental sesame oil
Watercress sprigs for garnish (optional)

1. With poultry or kitchen shears, remove backbones from hens by cutting along each side of backbone until it is freed. Place hens on work surface, skin side up, spread open, and, using mallet, pound breastbone so hen will lie flat.

2. Peel and mince garlic and ginger.

3. For marinade, combine garlic, soy sauce, peanut oil, sesame oil, ginger, and ¼ cup water in large shallow baking dish. Add hens and marinate, turning occasionally, at least 20 minutes.

4. Transfer hens to grill, place cut side down, and cook, turning frequently and basting with marinade, about 30 minutes, or until tender and juices run clear when hen is pierced with fork.

5. Reserve 3 tablespoons of marinade for carrots recipe and transfer remainder to small saucepan. Set on side of barbecue and bring to a simmer.

6. Transfer hens to individual plates and garnish with watercress sprigs, if desired. Pour warmed marinade into individual bowls and serve as dipping sauce for hens.

Stir-Fried Carrots with Snow Peas

3 carrots (about ¼ pound total weight)
½ cup water chestnuts, drained
½ pound snow peas
3 tablespoons reserved marinade from Cornish hens

1. Peel carrots and cut on diagonal into ⅛-inch-thick slices.

2. Cut water chestnuts into ¼-inch-thick slices.

3. Top, tail, and string snow peas. Wash snow peas under cold running water and pat dry with paper towels.

4. In wok or large heavy-gauge skillet, heat reserved marinade over medium-high heat. Add carrots and cook, covered, 3 minutes.

5. Uncover pan, add chestnuts and snow peas, and stir fry about 3 minutes, or until vegetables are just crisp-tender. Remove pan from heat.

Fresh Fruit in Cookie Cups

4 tablespoons unsalted butter
1 egg
½ cup confectioners' sugar
¼ cup ground walnuts
¼ cup all-purpose flour
2 tablespoons milk
1 teaspoon grated orange peel (optional)
3 cups summer berries (blueberries or raspberries), or
   3 cups cut-up fresh fruit of your choice (kiwis, grapes, orange sections, bananas, or papayas), or 4 scoops vanilla ice cream

1. Preheat oven to 375 degrees and generously grease 2 baking sheets with 2 tablespoons butter.

2. Separate egg, placing white in medium-size bowl. Reserve yolk for another use.

3. Beat egg white with whisk or with electric beater on medium speed, until foamy, about 1 minute. Add sugar, walnuts, flour, milk, remaining butter, and orange peel, if using, and, with wooden spoon, stir to combine.

4. Place 2 cookies on each baking sheet, using 1½ to 2 tablespoons batter per cookie and spreading it into 6-inch circles.

5. Bake first batch of 4 cookies, turning sheets from back to front once, 8 to 10 minutes, or until edges of cookies are browned. Remove from oven and repeat with second batch.

6. As soon as first batch of cookies is done, remove each cookie with metal spatula and drape over a custard cup. Push cookie into cup with your fingers, molding it to shape of cup (see illustration). Top of cookie will flute naturally.

Let stand 3 minutes. Remove cookies from custard cups and transfer to wire rack to cool. Repeat procedure with second batch of cookies.

7. Just before serving, fill each cookie with fruit of your choice or ice cream.

Grilled Monkfish with Lime-Butter Baste
Marinated Vegetables
Bulgur with Carrots and Scallions

On a large serving platter, form a bed with the bulgur and top it with the skewered monkfish sprinkled with chopped coriander or parsley and scallions, if desired. Serve the marinated vegetables in a large bowl.

Because the fish grills quickly for this backyard barbecue, have the bulgur cooking and the vegetables marinating before putting the skewers on the grill.

Because of its texture, monkfish is especially good for skewer cooking, as are the optional firm-fleshed catfish and large shrimp. Monkfish, also marketed as goosefish or anglerfish, is available on the Atlantic and Gulf Coasts, but is not widely marketed.

Bulgur, sometimes mistakenly called cracked wheat, consists of whole wheat berries that are crushed, steam cooked, and then dried. It is a traditional Middle Eastern grain with a nutty taste and crunchy texture. Because bulgur has been processed, it tends to get mushy if you add too much liquid or cook it too long.

WHAT TO DRINK

Iced tea would make a fine accompaniment to this meal. Alternatively, try a soft, dry white wine, either an Italian Soave or a California Chenin Blanc.

SHOPPING LIST AND STAPLES

2 pounds monkfish or catfish, skinned and cut into 2-inch chunks, or 24 large shrimp
2 medium-size carrots
¼ pound mushrooms
4 tomatoes
1 head leaf lettuce
1 bunch scallions
Small bunch coriander or parsley
4 small cloves garlic
2 lemons
5 limes
1 cup chicken broth, preferably homemade (see page 13), or canned
1 stick plus 2 tablespoons unsalted butter
¾ cup vegetable oil
2 tablespoons Dijon mustard
1 cup bulgur
1 teaspoon sugar (optional)
Salt and freshly ground black pepper

UTENSILS

Barbecue
Medium-size heavy-gauge saucepan with cover

Small saucepan
13 x 9 x 2-inch glass baking dish
Serving platter
Salad bowl
Small bowl
Salad spinner (optional)
Measuring cups and spoons
Chef's knife
Paring knife
Wooden spoon
Slotted spoon
Basting brush
Grater
Citrus juicer (optional)
Four 12-inch skewers
Vegetable peeler

START-TO-FINISH STEPS

1. Start barbecue.
2. Squeeze lemon juice for vegetables recipe and lime juice for vegetables and for monkfish recipes. Trim scallions, wash, and pat dry with paper towels. Cut 2 scallions into ¼-inch-thick rounds for vegetables recipe and chop 4 scallions for bulgur recipe.
3. Follow marinated vegetables recipe steps 1 and 2.
4. While vegetables are marinating, quarter limes, peel and devein shrimp, if using, and follow monkfish recipe steps 1 through 3.
5. Follow bulgur recipe steps 1 through 3.
6. Ten minutes before bulgur is done, follow monkfish recipe step 4, if cooking monkfish or catfish, or 8 minutes before it is done, if cooking shrimp.
7. While monkfish is grilling, wash lettuce and dry in salad spinner or pat dry with paper towels. Follow marinated vegetables recipe step 3.
8. Follow bulgur recipe step 4, monkfish recipe step 5, and serve with marinated vegetables.

RECIPES

Grilled Monkfish with Lime-Butter Baste

2 small cloves garlic
Small bunch coriander or parsley
1 stick unsalted butter
2 tablespoons lime juice
½ teaspoon salt
2 limes, quartered
2 pounds monkfish or catfish, cut into 2-inch chunks (about 24 pieces), or 24 large shrimp

1. Peel and mince garlic. Wash and pat dry coriander or parsley. Finely chop enough coriander or parsley to measure 2 tablespoons plus 1 tablespoon for garnish, if using.
2. In small saucepan, combine garlic, butter, lime juice, and salt and heat over low heat, stirring occasionally with wooden spoon, until butter has melted. Off heat, stir in 2 tablespoons coriander or parsley.

3. On each of four 12-inch skewers, place 1 lime wedge, followed by 3 chunks of fish, another lime wedge, then 3 more chunks of fish, and finish the skewer with a lime wedge. Brush the fish with the melted lime butter.
4. Place skewers on grill set 4 inches from heat and cook, turning occasionally, 8 to 10 minutes (5 to 8 minutes for shrimp), or until fish flakes easily with tip of sharp knife (or until shrimp have firmed up and turned pinkish white).
5. Transfer skewers to platter with bulgur. Drizzle with remaining lime butter and sprinkle with 1 tablespoon chopped parsley or coriander.

Marinated Vegetables

2 small cloves garlic, peeled and crushed
¾ cup vegetable oil
¼ cup fresh lemon juice
¼ cup fresh lime juice
2 tablespoons Dijon mustard
1 teaspoon sugar (optional)
2 scallions, cut into ¼-inch-thick rounds
½ tablespoon salt
Freshly ground black pepper
4 tomatoes, cored and thickly sliced
¼ pound mushrooms, thickly sliced
1 head leaf lettuce

1. In small bowl, combine garlic, oil, citrus juices, mustard, sugar, if using, scallions, salt, and pepper to taste and stir with fork until blended.
2. In shallow glass baking dish, arrange tomatoes and mushrooms in a single layer. Pour dressing over vegetables and marinate, turning vegetables occasionally, at least 30 minutes.
3. Just before serving, line salad bowl with lettuce. With slotted spoon, transfer tomatoes and mushrooms to lettuce-lined bowl. Spoon marinade over vegetables and sprinkle with a few grindings of black pepper, if desired.

Bulgur with Carrots and Scallions

2 medium-size carrots
2 tablespoons unsalted butter
1 cup bulgur
4 scallions, chopped
1 cup chicken stock
¼ teaspoon freshly ground black pepper
Salt

1. Peel carrots and, using large holes of grater, shred or cut carrots into ⅛-inch julienne.
2. In medium-size heavy-gauge saucepan, melt butter over medium heat. Add carrot and sauté, stirring frequently, about 3 minutes. Add bulgur and scallions, and stir until evenly coated with butter. Add stock, 1 cup water, pepper, and salt to taste and stir to combine.
3. Bring mixture to a boil over medium-high heat. Reduce heat to a simmer, cover, and cook until bulgur is tender, 10 to 15 minutes.
4. Fluff bulgur with fork and turn onto serving platter.

Great Grilled Burgers
Raw Vegetables with Creamy Basil Dip
Fruit Layers with Vanilla Sauce

This casual barbecue consists of raw vegetables with a dip, hamburgers in one (or all) of three variations, and a fruit dessert.

This barbecue is easy to organize: Have the raw vegetables with their dip and the fruit dessert ready and chilling before you grill the burgers. The main hamburger recipe calls for scallions, freshly ground pepper, and other seasonings. If you want to make the Mexican version, you will need a can of chilies and some chili powder. For the French variation, be sure you have some Burgundy wine and dried thyme on hand.

WHAT TO DRINK

Best bet with this straightforward menu would be ice-cold beer or ale. If you want wine, choose a simple red—a Beaujolais or a young, fruity Zinfandel.

SHOPPING LIST AND STAPLES

1½ pounds ground beef
1 yellow squash
2 carrots
Large cucumber
2 red bell peppers
¼ pound mushrooms
Small bunch scallions
Medium-size bunch basil, or medium-size bunch parsley
   plus 2 tablespoons dried basil
Small clove garlic
½ to ⅔ pound seedless red grapes
1 canteloupe, or ½ honeydew or other melon

3 kiwi
3 nectarines, apples, or pears
½ pint sour cream
1 cup vanilla yogurt
¼ pound Cheddar, Jarlsberg, Muenster, or blue cheese
¼ pound Parmesan cheese
1 tablespoon cider vinegar
⅓ cup good-quality commercial mayonnaise
¼ cup Worcestershire sauce
1 loaf French or Italian bread
Salt and freshly ground pepper
2 tablespoons orange-flavored liqueur

UTENSILS

Barbecue
Food processor or blender
Platter
Medium-size bowl
Medium-size glass serving bowl
2 small serving bowls
Measuring cups and spoons
Chef's knife
Paring knife
Long-handled metal spatula
Rubber spatula
Melon baller
Vegetable peeler

START-TO-FINISH STEPS

1. Follow fruit layers recipe steps 1 through 3.
2. Start barbecue.
3. Follow vegetables recipe steps 1 through 3.
4. Follow burgers recipe steps 1 through 4 or make burger variation of your choice.
5. Follow burgers recipe step 5 and serve with vegetables and dip.
6. For dessert, serve fruit layers with vanilla sauce.

RECIPES

Great Grilled Burgers

1½ pounds ground beef
2 scallions, thinly sliced
¼ cup Worcestershire sauce
1½ teaspoons salt
Freshly ground pepper
8 slices French or Italian bread
¼ pound Cheddar, Jarlsberg, or Muenster, shredded, or
    ¼ pound blue cheese, crumbled

1. In medium-size bowl, combine beef with scallions, Worcestershire sauce, and salt.
2. Shape meat into 4 patties, each about ¾ inch thick. Generously coat both sides of patties with pepper.
3. Place on grill and cook, turning once, to desired degree of doneness.

4. Five minutes before burgers are done, place bread on grill and toast about 2 minutes per side.
5. Transfer toasted bread to platter. With metal spatula, place 1 burger on each of 4 bread slices, top with cheese and remaining bread, and serve.

Burger Variations

Mexican Burgers: Combine ground beef with 1 teaspoon drained, chopped chilies, 1½ teaspoons chili powder, and ½ teaspoon salt and proceed as for Great Grilled Burgers. Serve on toasted English muffins, topped with lettuce, tomato, avocado, and sour cream.

French Burgers: Combine ground beef with ¼ cup Burgundy, 1 teaspoon dried thyme, and ½ teaspoon salt and proceed as for Great Grilled Burgers. Serve on toasted slices of French or Italian bread, topped with 2 cups chopped onions and 1 cup sliced mushrooms that have been sautéed in 2 tablespoons unsalted butter.

Raw Vegetables with Creamy Basil Dip

¼ pound mushrooms
Large cucumber, cut into ½-inch julienne
2 red bell peppers, cut into ½-inch julienne
2 carrots, peeled and cut into ½-inch julienne
1 yellow squash, cut into ½-inch-thick rounds
1 cup fresh basil leaves, or 1 cup parsley leaves plus
    2 tablespoons dried basil, crushed
Small clove garlic, peeled and minced
1 cup sour cream
⅓ cup mayonnaise
2 tablespoons grated Parmesan cheese
1 tablespoon cider vinegar
¼ teaspoon freshly ground pepper
Salt

1. Wipe mushrooms with damp paper towels.
2. Arrange vegetables on platter, cover, and refrigerate.
3. In food processor or blender, combine fresh basil or parsley and dried basil, garlic, and remaining ingredients, and process until smooth. Scrape into small serving bowl, cover, and chill at least 45 minutes.

Fruit Layers with Vanilla Sauce

1 cup vanilla yogurt
2 tablespoons orange-flavored liqueur
1 cantaloupe, or ½ honeydew or other melon
3 kiwis, peeled and cut into rounds
3 nectarines, apples, or pears, sliced
½ to ⅔ pound seedless red grapes, stemmed

1. In small serving bowl, combine yogurt and liqueur, and stir until blended. Cover and chill at least 1 hour.
2. Halve melon, scoop out seeds, and discard. With melon baller, scoop out melon balls.
3. In medium-size glass serving bowl or carrying container, form individual layers of each fruit, adding them in the order listed. Cover and chill at least 45 minutes or until ready to serve.

Ron Davis

MENU 1 (Left)
Duck, Chicken, and Veal Salad
Pasta with Three Cheeses
Asparagus with Garlic Dressing

MENU 2
Grilled Bluefish with Spinach, Bread,
and Vegetable Stuffing
Tomato, Onion, and Arugula Salad
Leeks with Roasted Pepper and Bûcheron Cheese

MENU 3
Scallop Seviche
Sweet-and-Spicy Barbecued Spareribs
Honey-Mustard Coleslaw

Ron Davis has his own basic motto for successful cooking: "Simplicity creates elegance." He uses only the highest-quality products prepared to preserve their natural flavors. To do this, he avoids intricate seasonings and complex sauces that mask flavors. The barbecued bluefish of Menu 2, with a fresh sautéed spinach and bread stuffing, for example, is enhanced by basting during cooking with the pan drippings from the sautéed spinach. Menu 1 features another straightforward approach. Strips of duck, chicken, and veal are first sautéed, then combined with raw vegetables and dressed with a lemon-, garlic-, and mustard-based mixture. He accompanies the meat with a chilled pasta dish—spirals and shells dressed with Roquefort, Parmesan, and Romano cheeses.

Ron Davis describes himself as an American cook who draws upon all the available influences, and Menu 3 is an example of how he structures an American meal: the spareribs are Southwestern, and the scallop seviche, Mexican.

Organize this elegant picnic in three wicker baskets: in one, put the duck, chicken, and veal salad; in the second, the pasta salad with cheese dressing; and in the third, the bundled asparagus spears with garlic dressing.

Duck, Chicken, and Veal Salad
Pasta with Three Cheeses
Asparagus with Garlic Dressing

This picnic features two main-dish salads. Chill the two salad dressings and the garlic dip for the asparagus spears while you prepare the rest of the meal. Combine the pasta and the meat salads with their respective dressings, then pack the meat salad and the asparagus dip in an ice chest for transporting to the picnic. You must do this to keep the egg-based dressings chilled.

WHAT TO DRINK

For a red wine, try a young Zinfandel or Chianti; for white, a California Sauvignon Blanc or an Italian Chardonnay.

SHOPPING LIST AND STAPLES

1 breast of duck, boned and skinned
2 whole chicken breasts, boned and skinned
1 pound veal scaloppine, pounded to ⅛-inch thickness
1 to 1½ pounds asparagus spears of uniform size
Small head broccoli (optional)
Small onion
3 stalks celery
Medium-size red bell pepper
12 cherry tomatoes (optional)
5 large mushrooms
Small bunch parsley
Small bunch dill
Small bunch basil
1 small shallot
3 cloves garlic
1 lemon
2 eggs
½ pint sour cream
4 tablespoons unsalted butter
¼ pound Roquefort cheese
2 ounces Parmesan cheese
2 ounces Romano cheese
¾ cup olive oil, approximately
⅔ cup vegetable oil
2 tablespoons plus 1 teaspoon red wine vinegar
⅓ cup mayonnaise
½ teaspoon Dijon mustard
6-ounce can pitted black olives (optional)
½ pound small pasta shells
½ pound small pasta spirals
⅓ cup flour
Salt

Freshly ground white pepper
Freshly ground black pepper
Cayenne pepper
¼ cup dry white wine or dry vermouth

UTENSILS

Food processor or blender
Large skillet
Large saucepan or stockpot with cover
Small saucepan
Large sauté pan
Medium-size sauté pan
2 large bowls
Medium-size mixing bowl
2 small bowls
Strainer
Colander
Measuring cups and spoons
Chef's knife
Paring knife
2 wooden spoons
Whisk (if not using mixer)
Electric mixer (optional)
2 large plastic carrying containers with lids
1 small jar with lid

START-TO-FINISH STEPS

1. Follow pasta recipe step 1.
2. While water is coming to a boil, prepare herbs and juice lemon. Grate Parmesan and Romano, and combine in small bowl.
3. Follow pasta recipe steps 2 through 8.
4. Follow salad recipe steps 1 through 5.
5. Follow asparagus recipe steps 1 through 5.
6. Follow salad recipe steps 6 and 7.
7. Follow pasta recipe step 9, salad recipe step 8, and pack with asparagus and dressing.
8. Before serving, toss salads and stir dressing.

RECIPES

Duck, Chicken, and Veal Salad

1 breast of duck, boned and skinned
2 whole chicken breasts, boned and skinned
1 pound veal scaloppine, pounded to ⅛-inch thickness
⅓ cup all-purpose flour

4 tablespoons olive oil
1 tablespoon unsalted butter
¼ cup dry white wine or dry vermouth
Medium-size red bell pepper
3 stalks celery
Small onion
2 tablespoons chopped parsley
1 tablespoon chopped dill
Salt and freshly ground white pepper
Salad dressing (see following recipe)

1. Cut duck, chicken, and veal into strips.
2. Dredge veal lightly with flour.
3. In large sauté pan, heat 2 tablespoons olive oil over medium heat. Add veal strips and sauté 3 to 4 minutes.
4. Drain veal in colander and then transfer to large bowl.
5. In same sauté pan, heat butter and remaining olive oil over medium heat. Add poultry strips and sauté 4 to 5 minutes. Just before removing from heat, add wine or vermouth and toss strips until evenly coated. Drain in colander and transfer to bowl with veal.
6. Core, seed, and halve red pepper. Cut pepper and celery into ¼-inch dice. Peel and dice onion.
7. Add vegetables to veal and poultry strips and, with wooden spoon, toss gently to combine. Add parsley, dill, salt, and white pepper to taste, and toss.
8. Pour dressing over salad and toss to coat. Turn into large carrying container with lid.

Salad Dressing

2 egg yolks
Juice of ½ lemon
2 tablespoons red wine vinegar
¼ teaspoon minced garlic, crushed
1 small shallot, minced
½ teaspoon Dijon mustard
Pinch of Cayenne pepper
Pinch of salt
⅓ cup olive oil
⅔ cup vegetable oil

1. In medium-size bowl, combine egg yolks, lemon juice, vinegar, garlic, shallot, mustard, Cayenne, and salt. With electric mixer at low speed or with whisk, beat briefly.
2. In measuring cup, combine olive oil and vegetable oil.
3. Beating constantly at low speed, slowly drizzle oil into yolk mixture. Increase speed to medium and beat steadily until dressing is thick and smooth.
4. Cover and refrigerate until ready to pack.

Pasta with Three Cheeses

Salt
5 large mushrooms
½ pound small pasta shells
½ pound small pasta spirals
½ teaspoon minced garlic, crushed
3 tablespoons chopped basil
4 tablespoons olive oil

1 tablespoon chopped parsley
Juice of ½ lemon
1 teaspoon red wine vinegar
1 cup broccoli florets (optional)
12 cherry tomatoes (optional)
1 cup pitted black olives (optional)
3 tablespoons unsalted butter
¼ teaspoon freshly ground black pepper
¼ pound Roquefort cheese, crumbled
2 ounces freshly grated Parmesan cheese
2 ounces freshly grated Romano cheese

1. In large saucepan or stockpot, bring 4 teaspoons salt and 4 quarts cold water to a boil.
2. Cut mushrooms into ¼-inch-thick slices.
3. Cook pasta according to package directions, adding shells 4 minutes after adding spirals.
4. While pasta is cooking, combine garlic, basil, oil, parsley, lemon juice, and vinegar in bowl of processor or blender and process about 1 minute, or until smooth. Cover bowl and refrigerate until ready to pack picnic.
5. If using broccoli, bring 1 quart water and 1 teaspoon salt to a boil in small saucepan. Add florets and blanch 1 minute. Turn into colander, refresh under cold running water, and drain. Halve tomatoes, if using. In large bowl, combine broccoli, tomatoes, and olives, if using.
6. In colander, drain pasta and rinse under cold running water. Refill pan with cold water and return pasta to pan.
7. In medium-size sauté pan, melt butter over medium heat. Add mushrooms and pepper, and sauté 3 to 4 minutes.
8. Drain cooled pasta thoroughly and add to vegetables.
9. Add cheeses to pasta mixture and toss to combine. Add dressing and toss gently until evenly coated. Turn into large carrying container with lid.

Asparagus with Garlic Dressing

Salt
1 to 1½ pounds asparagus spears of uniform size
⅓ cup mayonnaise
⅔ cup sour cream
½ teaspoon minced garlic
1 tablespoon chopped parsley
¼ teaspoon freshly ground white pepper
Pinch of Cayenne pepper

1. Break off tough bottom stems of asparagus spears. Wash asparagus and gently pat dry with paper towels.
2. In large skillet, bring 1 teaspoon salt and 2 inches of water to a rolling boil.
3. While water is heating, combine remaining ingredients and salt to taste in small bowl, and stir until blended. Transfer dressing to jar with lid or other carrying container and refrigerate until ready to pack picnic.
4. Add asparagus to boiling water and cook, uncovered, just until bright green and crisp-tender, 1 to 2 minutes.
5. In colander, drain asparagus and leave under cold running water until completely cool, about 3 minutes. Drain and pat dry. Wrap securely in plastic wrap.

Grilled Bluefish with Spinach, Bread, and Vegetable Stuffing
Tomato, Onion, and Arugula Salad
Leeks with Roasted Pepper and Bûcheron Cheese

A whole bluefish looks dramatic in any setting. Here it is gar-
nished with sliced tomatoes, lemons, and watercress sprigs.
Leeks with red peppers and Bûcheron and the salad are served
in separate containers.

S ince you will be cooking the fish last for this barbecue, dress the leeks and the salad just before the fish is ready to be served.

Bluefish, an abundant East Coast species, has oily flesh that requires little extra oil or fat during cooking. If bluefish is not available, substitute red fish or river trout. Stuffed with a spinach filling, then tied up for barbecuing, the bluefish cooks over the hot coals in a hinged wire basket that closes tightly around the fish and prevents it from breaking apart and falling into the fire. You can easily turn the long-handled basket to control the speed at which the fish cooks. If you have no basket, you can wrap the fish in foil and cook it on the grill, but the skin will not get crisp.

WHAT TO DRINK

These sharp, clear flavors need a firm, dry white wine: A California Chardonnay, an Alsatian Sylvaner, or a white Graves are all good choices.

SHOPPING LIST AND STAPLES

3-pound whole bluefish, dressed and boned
1½ pounds tomatoes plus 1 tomato (optional)
¼ pound fresh cultivated mushrooms
Medium-size red bell pepper
Medium-size yellow onion
Small red onion
4 small leeks
¾ pound spinach
Small head red or green leaf lettuce
Small bunch watercress (optional)
2 bunches arugula or watercress
Small bunch fresh parsley
Small bunch fresh dill
Small bunch fresh basil, or ½ teaspoon dried
1 shallot
3 cloves garlic
2 medium-size lemons plus additional lemon (optional)
Medium-size navel orange
1 egg
2½ tablespoons unsalted butter
2 ounces Bûcheron cheese (or any sharp chèvre or feta cheese)
7-ounce jar roasted red peppers

¾ cup blended oil (any oil but olive)
¼ cup red wine vinegar
1 teaspoon tamari, or ½ teaspoon soy sauce
4 teaspoons Dijon mustard
5 slices white or whole-wheat bread (about 4 ounces)
1 teaspoon sesame seeds
Salt
Freshly ground pepper
½ cup dry white wine

UTENSILS

Barbecue
Hinged grill basket
Medium-size skillet with cover
Small heavy-gauge skillet
Small saucepan (for clarifying butter)
Large sauté pan
Large salad bowl
3 medium-size bowls
2 small bowls
3 small jars with lids or other carrying containers
2 platters
Salad spinner (optional)
Colander
Strainer
Measuring cups and spoons
Chef's knife
Paring knife
2 wooden spoons
Slotted spoon
Whisk
20 inches thin cord

START-TO-FINISH STEPS

Thirty minutes ahead: Make clarified butter (see page 15).

1. Start barbecue.
2. Peel, mince, and crush garlic for all recipes. Peel, mince, and crush shallot for leeks recipe. Wash, pat dry, and chop parsley, dill, and fresh basil, if using, for bluefish. Juice lemons for all recipes. Follow bluefish recipe steps 1 through 3.
3. While vegetable mixture is cooking, follow leeks recipe steps 1 and 2.
4. Follow bluefish recipe step 4.
5. While spinach is cooking, follow salad recipe step 1.

6. Follow bluefish recipe step 5 and leeks recipe step 3.
7. While leeks are poaching, follow salad recipe steps 2 and 3.
8. Follow leeks recipe steps 4 through 7 and salad recipe steps 4 through 7.
9. Follow bluefish recipe steps 6 through 10.
10. Follow salad recipe step 8 and leeks recipe step 8.
11. When barbecue is ready, follow bluefish recipe step 11.
12. Five minutes before fish is done, follow salad recipe step 9 and leeks recipe step 9.
13. Follow bluefish recipe steps 12 and 13, and serve with salad and leeks.

RECIPES

Grilled Bluefish with Spinach, Bread, and Vegetable Stuffing

¾ pound spinach
Medium-size red bell pepper
Medium-size yellow onion
½ pound tomatoes, plus one for garnish (optional)
¼ pound fresh cultivated mushrooms
2 tablespoons clarified butter
¾ teaspoon minced garlic
Juice of 1 medium-size lemon
1 teaspoon chopped fresh parsley
1 teaspoon chopped fresh dill
1½ teaspoons chopped basil, or ½ teaspoon dried
½ cup dry white wine
Watercress sprigs for garnish (optional)
1 lemon for garnish (optional)
5 slices white or whole-wheat bread (about 4 ounces)
1 egg
Salt and freshly ground pepper
3-pound bluefish, dressed and boned

1. In colander, wash spinach thoroughly under cold running water. Dry in salad spinner or pat dry with paper towels. Chop coarsely into 1-inch-wide strips.
2. Wash red pepper and pat dry with paper towels. Core, seed, and halve pepper. Cut into ¼- to ½-inch dice. Peel onion and dice. Wash tomatoes and pat dry with paper towels. Slice one for garnish, if using. Core, halve and seed remaining tomatoes, and cut into ¼- to ½-inch dice. Wipe mushrooms with damp paper towels and cut into ¼-inch-thick slices.

41

3. In large sauté pan, heat clarified butter over medium high heat. Add red pepper, tomatoes, mushrooms, garlic, lemon juice, parsley, dill, and basil. Sauté mixture, stirring frequently with wooden spoon, about 5 minutes.

4. Add spinach and wine, and stir to combine. Cook spinach, stirring frequently, until wilted but still bright green, about 5 minutes.

5. Set strainer over medium-size bowl. Turn spinach mixture into strainer and drain thoroughly. Transfer vegetable liquid to jar with lid or other carrying container for transport.

6. Prepare garnishes, if using: Wash watercress and dry in salad spinner or pat dry with paper towels; wash tomato, pat dry, and cut crosswise into ¼-inch-thick slices; cut lemon into ⅛-inch-thick slices. Wrap in plastic for transport.

7. With your fingers, tear bread into ½- to ¾-inch pieces and place in medium-size mixing bowl. Add drained vegetable mixture and toss to combine.

8. In small bowl, beat egg with fork. Add egg to stuffing mixture and stir until blended. Add salt and pepper to taste. If mixture seems dry, add a little of the reserved vegetable liquid and stir until incorporated. Mixture should be just barely wet enough to hold together.

9. Spread bluefish open and fill cavity with stuffing. Do not overfill; stuffing will expand during cooking.

10. Use cord to tie fish securely but not too tightly. Strips of foil may be used instead of cord. Wrap fish in aluminum foil for transport.

11. Unwrap fish and place in grilling basket. Set basket on hot grill 4 inches from heat and cook about 25 minutes, or until fish is flaky but still moist, reversing basket several times to grill both sides of fish evenly. Through basket, baste frequently with vegetable liquids.

12. Remove fish from grill. Open basket, lay platter over side of basket that contains fish, and invert so that fish drops onto platter. Cut strings tying fish, remove, and discard.

13. Serve the fish garnished with watercress sprigs, tomato, and lemon slices, if desired.

Tomato, Onion, and Arugula Salad

2 bunches fresh arugula or watercress
Small red onion
1 teaspoon sesame seeds
Medium-size navel orange
1 pound tomatoes
Salt and freshly ground pepper
2 tablespoons red wine vinegar
1 teaspoon tamari, or ½ teaspoon soy sauce
Juice of ½ medium-size lemon
¼ cup blended oil (any oil but olive)

1. Place greens in medium-size bowl, add cold water to cover, and let greens soak 5 minutes.

2. Remove greens from bowl, shake off excess water, and dry in salad spinner or pat dry with paper towels. Remove stems and discard.

3. Peel onion and cut into ⅛-inch-thick slices. Set aside.

4. In small heavy-gauge skillet, toast sesame seeds over medium heat, shaking skillet frequently to keep seeds from scorching, until they turn golden brown and release their fragrance, about 3 to 4 minutes.

5. With paring knife, trim peel and white pith from orange. Then, over salad bowl, holding orange in one hand and knife in other, free segments by cutting toward center on each side of membranes, letting segments fall into bowl.

6. Wash tomatoes and pat dry with paper towels. Core tomatoes and, with chef's knife, chop coarsely into 1-inch chunks. Place chunks in salad bowl.

7. Add sliced onion to tomatoes and mix until onions are evenly distributed. Add arugula or watercress, orange sections, sesame seeds, and salt and pepper to taste, and toss to combine. Cover with plastic wrap and refrigerate until ready to leave.

8. For dressing, combine vinegar, tamari or soy, lemon juice, and oil in small jar with lid or other carrying container.

9. Just before serving, shake or stir dressing to recombine. Pour dressing over salad and toss gently.

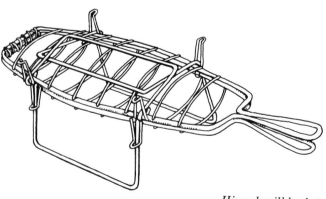

Hinged grill basket

Leeks with Roasted Pepper and Bûcheron

Salt
4 small leeks
7-ounce jar roasted red peppers
Small head red or green leaf lettuce
¼ cup crumbled Bûcheron cheese or any sharp chèvre or feta cheese
1 shallot, minced
½ teaspoon minced garlic
4 teaspoons Dijon mustard
2 tablespoons red wine vinegar
Juice of ½ medium-size lemon
¼ teaspoon freshly ground black pepper
½ cup blended oil (any oil but olive)

1. In medium-size skillet, bring enough water to cover leeks plus 1 teaspoon salt per 4 cups of water to a boil.
2. With chef's knife, trim leeks, leaving approximately 2 inches of green. Split leeks lengthwise, spread leaves, and wash thoroughly in cold water.
3. Add leeks to boiling water, reduce heat to a simmer, cover, and cook until leeks are tender, 6 to 7 minutes.
4. With slotted spoon, transfer leeks to colander and refresh under cold running water.
5. In strainer, rinse roasted peppers under cold running water. Chop enough pepper to measure ¼ cup. Set aside.
6. Remove outer leaves from lettuce, discarding any that are badly bruised and reserving inside leaves for another use. Wash leaves under cold running water and dry in salad spinner or pat dry with paper towels.
7. On platter, arrange a bed of lettuce leaves. Top with leeks and sprinkle with crumbled Bûcheron and chopped pepper. Cover with plastic wrap and refrigerate.
8. In small bowl, combine shallot, garlic, mustard, vinegar, lemon juice, and pepper. Beating constantly with whisk, add oil in a slow, steady stream, and beat until oil is totally incorporated. Transfer mixture to small jar with lid or other carrying container.
9. Just before serving, shake or stir dressing to recombine and pour over salad.

ADDED TOUCH

This old-fashioned crumb-topped apple pie is delicious served with pouring cream or whipped cream. If you are transporting it in hot weather, you may wish to accompany this dessert with sharp Cheddar cheese instead.

Apple Crumb Pie

1 cup sifted all-purpose flour plus ¾ cup sifted all-purpose or whole-wheat flour
¾ teaspoon salt
3 sticks chilled unsalted butter
1 lemon
2 pounds tart eating apples
1 cup firmly packed dark brown sugar
½ teaspoon freshly grated nutmeg
½ teaspoon cinnamon
1 cup heavy cream (optional)

1. Preheat oven to 350 degrees.
2. Sift together 1 cup flour and ½ teaspoon salt. Set aside.
3. Line counter or cutting board with several sheets of wax paper. With chef's knife, cut sticks of butter lengthwise in half and then in half again. Keeping quarters in stick form, make 8 crosswise slices through each stick, so it is divided into 32 little cubes. Separate cubes.
4. In medium-size bowl, combine 1 cubed stick of butter with flour-salt mixture and refrigerate remaining butter.
5. With pastry blender or two knives, cut butter into flour until mixture resembles coarse meal. Add 2 to 3 tablespoons cold water or just enough to make mixture cohere without becoming sticky. Form mixture into ball.
6. Lightly flour rolling surface and rolling pin. Roll dough out into circle large enough to fit 9-inch pie plate. Gently fold dough in half and then into quarters. Carefully transfer dough to pie plate and unfold, lining plate.
7. Juice lemon and set aside.
8. Peel, halve, and core apples. With chef's knife, cut each half into ½-inch-thick crescents and place in large mixing bowl. Add reserved lemon juice and toss until coated.
9. Arrange apple crescents in crust-lined pie plate.
10. Wipe out bowl with paper towels and into it sift remaining flour, brown sugar, and ¼ teaspoon salt. Remove remaining butter from refrigerator and add to bowl. Using pastry blender or 2 knives, cut butter into mixture until it is crumbly and well-combined.
11. Sprinkle apples with nutmeg and cinnamon, and then with crumb mixture. Do not combine.
12. Bake pie 45 minutes.
13. Serve hot or cold with pouring cream or whipped cream, if desired. If serving whipped cream, chill bowl and beaters for ten minutes. Pour cream into bowl and beat at slow and then medium speed until a spoonful is thick enough just to hold a shape, 3 to 4 minutes.

Scallop Seviche
Sweet-and-Spicy Barbecued Spareribs
Honey-Mustard Coleslaw

Because the spareribs need frequent basting while they grill, prepare the coleslaw and scallop seviche completely ahead of time. To ready the spareribs for the barbecue, you need to precook them either the night before the barbecue or 1 hour ahead. Not only does this shorten barbecuing time, it also prevents the meat from toughening on the hot grill.

The citrus juices in the seviche perform two functions: The acid of the lime juice "cooks" the scallops, and the lemon juice preserves the color of the avocado.

The colorful coleslaw, served in a large salad bowl, is a prominent part of this barbecue. Offer the scallop and avocado seviche as an appetizer or serve it as an accompaniment to the spareribs.

WHAT TO DRINK

Ice-cold beer or ale is a classic accompaniment to spareribs. You might like to try a dark English ale here. For wine, choose a good Gewürztraminer from Alsace or California, lightly chilled.

SHOPPING LIST AND STAPLES

2 racks spareribs (about 6 pounds total weight)
1 pound bay scallops, preferably, or 1 pound sea scallops
3 pounds Italian plum tomatoes
Medium-size avocado
½ pound white cabbage
½ pound red cabbage

Small zucchini
Small carrot
Medium-size onion
Small bunch spinach or small head Romaine
Small bunch parsley
Small bunch dill
Small bunch coriander
1 shallot
2 small cloves garlic
2 lemons
6 limes
1 stick unsalted butter
6-ounce can tomato paste
8-ounce jar small sweet gherkins
1 tablespoon red wine vinegar
1 tablespoon white wine vinegar
⅔ cup good-quality commercial mayonnaise
¼ cup prepared honey-mustard (or equal parts Dijon
    mustard and honey)
⅓ cup liquid brown sugar or dark cane syrup, or 3 table-
    spoons brown sugar plus ½ teaspoon maple syrup
¼ teaspoon ground cumin
½ teaspoon chili powder
½ teaspoon Cayenne pepper
Salt and freshly ground black pepper
⅓ cup dry red wine

UTENSILS

Food processor or grater
Blender
Large stockpot with cover
Large saucepan with cover
2 large mixing bowls
Medium-size bowl
Small bowl plus one additional (if preparing your own
    honey-mustard)
Salad spinner (optional)
Colander
Measuring cups and spoons
Chef's knife
Paring knife
Wooden spoon
Slotted spoon
Long-handled basting brush (optional)
Juicer

START-TO-FINISH STEPS

The night before or 1 hour ahead: In large covered stockpot, bring 5 quarts water to a boil. Add ribs to boiling
water, cover, and cook 25 minutes. Drain and pat dry.
Refrigerate overnight or proceed with recipe.

Thirty minutes ahead: Start barbecue.

1. Wash, pat dry, and chop parsley for all recipes. Wash, pat dry, and chop coriander for seviche. Juice lemons for all recipes. Juice limes for seviche. If using sea scallops, quarter them and follow seviche recipe steps 1 through 4.
2. Follow ribs recipe steps 1 through 3.
3. While barbecue sauce is simmering, follow coleslaw recipe steps 1 through 7.
4. Follow ribs recipe steps 4 through 6.
5. Ten minutes before ribs are done, while continuing to baste and turn ribs, follow seviche recipe step 5 and serve.
6. Follow ribs recipe step 7 and serve with coleslaw.

RECIPES
Scallop Seviche

1 pound bay scallops, preferably, or 1 pound sea scallops quartered
½ to ⅔ cup lime juice
¼ cup chopped parsley
⅓ cup chopped coriander
Medium-size avocado
2 tablespoons lemon juice
Small bunch spinach or small head Romaine lettuce

1. In medium-size bowl, combine scallops and enough lime juice to cover. Add parsley and coriander, and toss gently with wooden spoon to combine.
2. With paring knife, peel avocado. Cut in half lengthwise and separate by gently twisting halves in opposite directions. Remove pit and dice avocado into pieces approximately the same size as the scallops. In small bowl, combine avocado with lemon juice and toss gently until well coated. Let stand 5 minutes.
3. While avocado is marinating, place spinach in colander, wash thoroughly under cold running water, and dry in salad spinner or pat dry with paper towels. Remove stems and discard. If using Romaine, remove and discard any tough or discolored outer leaves. Wash, dry, and trim. Wrap greens in paper towels and refrigerate until needed.
4. With slotted spoon, transfer avocado to bowl with scallops and toss gently to combine. Cover and refrigerate about 30 minutes.
5. Line bowl or platter with spinach or lettuce leaves. With slotted spoon, transfer seviche to spinach- or lettuce-lined bowl and serve.

Sweet-and-Spicy Barbecued Spareribs

2 racks spare ribs (about 6 pounds total weight)
3 small cloves garlic
Medium-size onion
3 pounds Italian plum tomatoes
1 stick unsalted butter
¼ teaspoon ground cumin
½ teaspoon chili powder
1 tablespoon chopped parsley
½ teaspoon Cayenne pepper
¾ teaspoon freshly ground black pepper
1 tablespoon red wine vinegar
Juice of ½ lemon
6 ounces tomato paste
⅓ cup liquid brown sugar or dark cane syrup, or 3 tablespoons brown sugar plus ½ teaspoon maple syrup
⅓ cup dry red wine

1. Place grill 8 inches from coals and on it arrange pre-cooked ribs in single layer. Barbecue ribs, turning often with tongs or barbecue fork, 20 minutes, or until ribs lose their raw look.
2. Peel and chop garlic. Peel and coarsely chop onion. Wash tomatoes, pat dry with paper towels, core, and quarter.
3. In large saucepan, combine garlic, onion, tomatoes, butter, cumin, chili powder, parsley, Cayenne, black pepper, vinegar, and lemon juice. Bring to a simmer over low heat and, stirring occasionally with wooden spoon, simmer, covered, about 15 minutes.
4. Uncover pan and add tomato paste, liquid brown sugar or dark cane syrup (or brown sugar and maple syrup), and wine. Return to a simmer and cook, stirring, an additional 5 minutes, or until thick and smooth. Remove pan from heat.
5. Pour sauce into blender, 2 cups at a time, and blend until smooth, about 45 seconds. Transfer sauce to large mixing bowl. Repeat process until all of sauce has been puréed.
6. With long-handled basting brush or wooden spoon, baste ribs with barbecue sauce, turning frequently, until ribs are crusty with sauce and have turned a dark brick-red color, another 25 minutes.
7. Transfer ribs to platter and serve.

Honey-Mustard Coleslaw

½ pound white cabbage
½ pound red cabbage

Small zucchini
Small carrot
1 shallot
12 small sweet gherkins
Juice of 1 lemon
1 tablespoon white wine vinegar
1 tablespoon chopped dill
1 tablespoon chopped parsley
¼ cup prepared honey-mustard (or equal parts Dijon
  mustard and honey)
⅔ cup good-quality commercial mayonnaise
Salt and freshly ground pepper

1. Peel off tough outer leaves of cabbages and discard.
2. In food processor or on large holes of grater, thinly shred cabbages. Transfer to large mixing bowl and, with your hands, toss to mix colors. Wash zucchini and carrot and pat dry with paper towels.
3. Peel carrot. Shred zucchini and carrot in food processor or on large holes of grater.
4. Peel and mince shallot. Cut sweet gherkins into ¼- to ½-inch-thick slices.
5. Add vegetables, shallot, gherkins, lemon juice, vinegar, dill, and parsley to bowl with cabbages and, with your hands, toss to combine.
6. If making your own honey-mustard, combine 2 tablespoons Dijon mustard and 2 tablespoons honey in small bowl. Spoon mustard over slaw, add mayonnaise, and toss with salad server until blended. Add salt and pepper to taste and toss again.
7. Cover and chill thoroughly before serving.

ADDED TOUCH

The cook advises you not to bake this rich dark bread if the weather is rainy or very humid because the dough will not rise properly.

Black Bread

2 cups fine bread crumbs
4 tablespoons blackstrap molasses
4 teaspoons instant coffee
1 teaspoon sugar
½ teaspoon ground ginger
2 packages active dry yeast
4 tablespoons unsalted butter
3 cups rye flour
2 teaspoons salt

1¾ cups all-purpose flour
1 egg

1. Preheat oven to 350 degrees.
2. Spread bread crumbs in baking pan and toast in oven, shaking pan occasionally, until golden brown, 7 to 10 minutes.
3. Turn off oven, remove crumbs, and let cool.
4. In large mixing bowl, combine 2 cups hot water, molasses, and 3 teaspoons instant coffee, and stir until dissolved. Add cooled bread crumbs and stir until blended.
5. In small bowl, combine ½ cup lukewarm water, sugar, ginger, and yeast, and stir with fork until blended. Let stand about 15 minutes, or until mixture starts to foam.
6. In small saucepan, melt butter over low heat.
7. To form dough, add yeast mixture to molasses mixture and stir to combine. Slowly add rye flour, stirring with wooden spoon until completely incorporated. Add melted butter and salt, and stir until blended.
8. Turn 1½ cups all-purpose flour out onto large board. Place rye dough in center of flour and cover with inverted bowl. Let dough rest 15 minutes.
9. Uncover dough. Incorporating the all-purpose flour as you work, knead dough about 10 minutes, or until firm and no longer sticky.
10. Lightly butter large mixing bowl. Turn dough into bowl, cover with clean towel, and allow to rise in draft-free area until double in bulk, 1½ to 2 hours.
11. Lightly flour board. Turn dough out onto board and knead 5 minutes.
12. Butter baking pan and sprinkle with flour.
13. Shape dough into round or oblong loaf. Using your hands or 2 metal spatulas, carefully lift loaf onto baking sheet. Cover with towel and allow to rise until double in bulk, 30 to 60 minutes.
13. Preheat oven to 400 degrees.
15. Combine 1 teaspoon instant coffee with 3 tablespoons hot water in small bowl or cup and stir to dissolve. Set aside to cool.
16. In small bowl, beat egg lightly with fork. Add cooled instant-coffee mixture and beat lightly until combined.
17. With pastry brush, coat bread with coffee-egg glaze.
18. Place bread in oven and bake 40 to 45 minutes, or until bread has crisp crust and has a hollow sound when tapped with your fist.
19. Remove bread from oven and place on rack to cool. If packing up for picnic, cool at least 1 hour before wrapping in foil.

Victoria Wise

MENU 1 (Right)
Salmon Barbecued with Fennel,
Lemon, and Onion
Grilled Corn
Cucumbers and Radishes with Watercress

MENU 2
Grilled Rabbit
Grilled Yellow and Green Bell Peppers
Mediterranean Tomato Salad

MENU 3
Pork Loin Roasted with Garlic and Sage
Artichokes Oreganata
Tapénade

Victoria Wise spent her childhood in Japan and has lived in the south of France, where she apprenticed in a *charcuterie*—the French version of a delicatessen. This diverse background influences her cooking and menu planning. She uses classic French cooking techniques, yet she likes unorthodox combinations of flavors and ingredients. Today she works in California, where cooks have abundant seasonal produce and fresh aromatic herbs year round.

Californians love to barbecue, says Victoria Wise, and barbecuing is one of her specialties. For her grill, she routinely uses mesquite (page 11), which produces an intense, even heat. She describes Menu 1 as a typical West Coast barbecue with its mesquite fire and Pacific salmon. Her salmon recipe was inspired by the aromatic herb fennel. Victoria Wise says that the herb grows wild throughout California, but, if picking your own, be careful, as many poisonous plants resemble it.

Menu 2 shows southern European influences. A Mediterranean summer meal, it features grilled marinated rabbit accompanied by a Greek tomato salad and an Italian-style dish of grilled yellow and green peppers with olive oil and garlic.

Her third menu is Provençal: artichokes cooked with lemon, oregano, and garlic, and pork loin roasted with garlic and sage. Both are served with tapénade, a sauce containing capers whose name comes from the Provençal word for caper—*tapéno*.

A grilled salmon fillet, garnished with thin slices of lemon and a sprig of feathery fennel and served on a plank, is an impressive main course for this barbecue. With the grilled corn, offer guests an empty bowl for discarding the husks and silk. Serve the salad in individual bowls.

Salmon Barbecued with Fennel, Lemon, and Onion
Grilled Corn
Cucumbers and Radishes with Watercress

For this barbecue, first make the salad. Then, refrigerate the salad or store it in a chilled container while grilling the salmon and the corn.

The rich taste of the salmon is enhanced here by barbecuing over a mesquite fire. For further flavoring, it is grilled directly on top of stalks of fennel, an herb that is not widely available outside of California. Alternatively, buy the feathery top stalks of the vegetable fennel, or, if it, too, is unavailable, sprinkle fennel seeds on top of the fish or over the hot coals. You can also lay stalks of fresh dill under the grilling salmon, or sprinkle a combination of fennel seeds and dill on the salmon as it cooks.

WHAT TO DRINK

The best beverages for this menu are beer or iced tea. If you really prefer wine, try a dry and spicy California or Alsatian Gewürztraminer.

SHOPPING LIST AND STAPLES

2½-pound salmon fillet, about 1¾ inches thick at thickest point
6 to 8 ears tender young corn, unshucked
2 medium-size cucumbers (about 1 pound total weight)
1 bunch red radishes
Large bunch watercress
Medium-size onion
5 lemons
1 lime
Small bunch fresh parsley
6 fresh fennel stalks with greens (not bulbs) plus greens (optional), or small bunch fresh dill, preferably long-stemmed, or 2 teaspoons dried dill plus ½ teaspoon fennel seeds
1 stick unsalted butter, approximately
¼ cup plus 2 tablespoons olive oil
Salt and freshly ground black pepper

UTENSILS

Covered barbecue
Mesquite for barbecuing, if available
Medium-size bowl
Small bowl
Salad spinner (optional)
Measuring cups and spoons
Chef's knife
Paring knife
2 wooden spoons
Melon baller or teaspoon
2 metal spatulas
Juicer
Vegetable peeler
Instant-reading meat thermometer
Heatproof mitt

START-TO-FINISH STEPS

1. Start barbecue, using mesquite, if available.
2. Follow salad recipe steps 1 through 5.
3. Follow salmon recipe steps 1 through 5.
4. When coals are covered with white ash, place grill rack 4 inches from them and heat 2 to 3 minutes.
5. Follow corn recipe step 1 and salmon recipe step 6.
6. Follow salmon recipe step 7, corn recipe step 2, salad recipe step 6, and serve.

RECIPES

Salmon Barbecued with Fennel, Lemon, and Onion

2½-pound salmon fillet, about 1¾ inches thick at thickest point
3 tablespoons olive oil
Medium-size onion
3 lemons
6 fresh fennel stalks with greens (not bulbs) plus greens for garnish (optional), or small bunch fresh dill, preferably long-stemmed, or 2 teaspoons dried dill plus ½ teaspoon fennel seeds.
Salt and freshly ground black pepper

1. Wipe salmon with damp paper towels.
2. Spoon oil over salmon and, with your fingers, coat both sides evenly.
3. Peel onion and slice thinly.
4. Cut lemons into ⅛- to ¼-inch-thick slices. Wash fresh dill, if using, and pat dry.
5. Top salmon with single layer of onion slices and slices of 1 lemon. If using dried dill and fennel seeds, scatter over onion and lemon.
6. Lay fennel stalks or fresh dill on top of hot grill and place salmon on top of them. Cover barbecue with hood and cook with vent open 20 to 30 minutes, or until instant-

reading meat thermometer placed in thickest portion of salmon registers 115 degrees.

7. Using 2 metal spatulas, transfer salmon to cutting board or platter, sprinkle with salt and pepper to taste, and garnish with lemon slices and fennel greens, if desired.

Grilled Corn

6 to 8 ears tender young corn, unshucked
1 stick unsalted butter, approximately
Salt and freshly ground black pepper

1. Place unhusked corn on grill. Cover barbecue and cook corn with vent open, 30 minutes, turning occasionally.
2. Serve corn in husks, accompanied by butter, salt, and freshly ground black pepper.

Cucumbers and Radishes with Watercress

2 medium-size cucumbers (about 1 pound total weight)
1 bunch red radishes
6 sprigs parsley
Large bunch watercress
2 lemons
1 lime
¼ teaspoon salt
3 tablespoons olive oil

1. Wash cucumbers thoroughly and pat dry with paper towels. With vegetable peeler, remove alternate lengths of peel to create a striped effect. Halve cucumbers lengthwise and, if necessary, remove seeds with melon baller or teaspoon. Place cucumbers cut side down and, with chef's knife, cut into ½-inch-thick slices. Transfer slices to medium-size bowl.

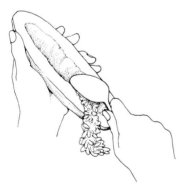

2. Trim radishes, wash, and pat dry with paper towels. With paring knife, cut into ½-inch-thick rounds. Add radishes to bowl.
3. Keeping parsley and watercress separate, remove stems, wash, and pat dry with paper towels. With chef's knife, mince parsley and add to bowl. Reserve watercress.
4. Juice lemons and lime. In small bowl, combine juices, salt, and olive oil, and stir with fork until blended.
5. Line small canning jars or small bowls with reserved watercress.
6. Pour dressing over salad and toss. Spoon salad into watercress-lined jars or bowls.

This berry tart can be flavored with Kirschwasser, a cherry-flavored brandy, or with another *eau de vie* (clear fruit brandy) such as Calvados, Poire Williams, or Mirabelle. Serve plain or with whipped cream or créme fraîche.

Berry Tart

7 tablespoons unsalted butter
1 cup plus 1 tablespoon sifted flour
2 tablespoons sugar
2 pints fresh berries
1 tablespoon lemon juice
1 cup red currant jelly
1½ tablespoons Kirschwasser, other *eau de vie*, or Port

1. Cut butter into 1-tablespoon pieces and allow to come to room temperature.
2. Sift flour and sugar together into medium-size bowl.
3. Add butter and, with your fingers, work into dry ingredients until mixture resembles coarse meal. Add 1 tablespoon cold water and work flour-butter mixture until you can gather it into a ball. If necessary, add a few extra drops of cold water very sparingly.
4. Wrap dough in plastic wrap and flatten slightly with your palm. Refrigerate dough at least 1 hour or overnight.
5. Remove dough from refrigerator and let stand at room temperature until malleable, about 1 hour. Or, soften partially by beating dough, still wrapped in plastic, with rolling pin, turning dough as you beat it. Then, leave dough to warm and soften.
6. When dough is malleable, line 9-inch tart mold with removable bottom by pressing dough evenly against bottom and sides. Refrigerate at least 30 minutes.
7. Preheat oven to 400 degrees.
8. Prick bottom of tart 5 or 6 times with fork. Place mold in oven and bake until crust is golden brown and cooked through, about 20 minutes. If bottom begins to puff during baking, prick it with fork a few more times.
9. Remove mold from oven and set on rack to cool.
10. In colander, rinse berries, hull if necessary, and gently dry with paper towels.
11. For glaze, combine lemon juice, red currant jelly, and kirschwasser, *eau de vie*, or Port in small saucepan. Stirring constantly with whisk, bring to a boil over medium heat. Lower heat to a simmer and reduce glaze until it registers 200 degrees on candy thermometer, about 3 minutes. Remove pan from heat.
12. With pastry brush, lightly paint bottom and sides of shell with glaze. Reserve remaining glaze.
13. Starting at center and working outward, arrange berries in tart shell. If using strawberries, place them hulled side down. Using pastry brush, spread remaining glaze evenly over berries.
14. Serve at room temperature or refrigerate for up to 3 hours.
15. To serve, support bottom of tart ring with your hand and pushing upward, gently separate tart from sides of ring. Place tart with ring bottom on serving plate.

Grilled Rabbit
Grilled Yellow and Green Bell Peppers
Mediterranean Tomato Salad

Serve the rabbit and the green and yellow peppers on the same plate. Offer the Mediterranean tomato salad separately.

Rabbit, an often-overlooked delicacy, tastes somewhat like chicken. Because its flesh is lean and delicate, rabbit is enhanced by marinating, as in this recipe. Do not cook rabbit directly over hot coals: Use a covered barbecue for indirect cooking and lay the rabbit pieces at the perimeter of the fire. Otherwise, the meat will dry out.

WHAT TO DRINK

These vivid, summery flavors interact well with a full-flavored dry red wine such as a Chianti Classico, a Gigondas, or even a Châteauneuf-du-Pape.

SHOPPING LIST AND STAPLES

Two 2½-to 3-pound rabbits, each cut into 6 pieces
1 pound firm ripe tomatoes
2 yellow bell peppers
2 green bell peppers
3 small hot red or green chili peppers, or 1 teaspoon hot red pepper flakes
12 cloves garlic
Large bunch watercress
Small bunch fresh basil or parsley
Small bunch fresh thyme, or 1 teaspoon dried

6-ounce package feta cheese, preferably Bulgarian
3½-ounce jar Niçoise, Greek, or oil-cured black olives
1½ cups soy sauce
1 cup plus 3 tablespoons red wine vinegar
1 cup plus 2 tablespoons olive oil
2 bay leaves
Salt and freshly ground pepper
1½ cups dry red wine

UTENSILS

Covered barbecue grill
Mesquite for barbecuing, if available
Small enamel-lined saucepan
17 x 11-inch glass or enamel-lined baking dish
2 small bowls
Salad spinner (optional)
Measuring cups and spoons
Chef's knife
Paring knife
Slotted spoon
Wooden spoon
Tongs
Instant-reading meat thermometer
Fire rake for barbecue
Heatproof mitt
Thin rubber gloves

START-TO-FINISH STEPS

1. Start barbecue, using mesquite, if available.
2. Follow rabbit recipe steps 1 through 3.
3. Follow peppers recipe steps 1 and 2.
4. Follow salad recipe steps 1 through 3.
5. Follow peppers recipe steps 3 and 4.
6. After 10 minutes, follow rabbit recipe step 4.
7. After 5 minutes, follow rabbit recipe step 5.
8. Follow peppers recipe steps 5 through 8.
9. Follow salad recipe step 4, rabbit recipe step 6, peppers recipe step 9, and serve.

RECIPES

Grilled Rabbit

6 cloves garlic
3 small hot red or green chili peppers, or 1 teaspoon hot red pepper flakes
1½ cups soy sauce
1½ cups dry red wine
1 cup red wine vinegar
6 branches fresh thyme, or 1 teaspoon dried
2 bay leaves
Two 2½- to 3-pound rabbits, each cut into 6 pieces

1. Peel and halve garlic.
2. Wearing rubber gloves, wash fresh chilies, if using. Pat dry with paper towels, stem, and chop coarsely.
3. In large glass or enamel-lined baking dish, combine garlic and chilies, or dried red pepper flakes, with soy sauce, wine, vinegar, thyme, and bay leaves. Add rabbit and marinate 15 minutes, turning occasionally.
4. With slotted spoon, transfer rabbit to center of grill. Reserve marinade. Cover barbecue and, with vent open, cook rabbit 20 to 30 minutes or until meat thermometer plunged into thickest part of flesh registers 120 degrees.
5. Transfer marinade to small enamel-lined saucepan. On grill, reduce 15 to 20 minutes, or until slightly thickened.
6. With tongs, divide rabbit among individual dinner plates and spoon reduced marinade over rabbit.

Grilled Yellow and Green Bell Peppers

6 cloves garlic
2 yellow bell peppers
2 green bell peppers
¼ cup olive oil
Salt and freshly ground black pepper

1. Peel and mince garlic, and transfer to small bowl.
2. Wash peppers and pat dry with paper towels.
3. When coals are covered by white ash, using rake, move coals to sides of barbecue, leaving space in center. Place grill 4 inches from coals and heat 3 to 4 minutes.
4. Place peppers around edge of grill and cook 20 to 30 minutes, turning often with tongs to make sure peppers char evenly. Yellow peppers will take about 5 minutes longer than green peppers.
5. Place peppers in paper bag, and roll up top to seal tightly. Let sit until cooled and moist, about 10 minutes.
6. Remove peppers from bag and rub gently with paper towel to remove charred skin.
7. For dressing, combine olive oil with garlic.
8. Core, quarter, and seed peppers.
9. Arrange peppers alongside rabbit, alternating yellow and green pieces. Spoon dressing over top, and season with salt and pepper to taste.

Mediterranean Tomato Salad

Large bunch watercress
2 tablespoons coarsely chopped fresh basil, preferably, or oregano, chervil, cilantro, or parsley
1 pound firm ripe tomatoes
⅓ cup Niçoise, Greek, or oil-cured black olives
⅓ cup feta cheese, preferably Bulgarian, crumbled
3 tablespoons red wine vinegar
¼ cup plus 2 tablespoons olive oil

1. Keeping watercress and basil or other herbs separate remove stems, wash, and dry in salad spinner or pat dry with paper towels. Divide watercress among 4 salad plates. Reserve basil.
2. Wash tomatoes and pat dry. Core tomatoes and cut into ½-inch-thick slices. Arrange slices on top of watercress.
3. Distribute olives and feta over tomato slices. Set aside and keep cool.
4. In small bowl, combine basil, vinegar, and olive oil, stirring with fork until blended. Spoon dressing over salad.

Pork Loin Roasted with Garlic and Sage
Artichokes Oreganata
Tapénade

When you serve this elegant picnic, arrange the pork loin slices and the artichokes on separate platters. Offer the tapénade in a pitcher with a spoon for ladling and serve the bread in a napkin-lined basket.

You can serve this meal as a picnic or as a barbecue, since the boneless pork roast can be either roasted or barbecued. If you cook the pork in the oven, slice it after it cools and then take it to your picnic wrapped in plastic or foil. For a barbecue, grill the pork just before mealtime, so it comes to the table hot.

The tapénade is a classic Provençale purée of black olives, garlic, anchovies, and capers. It is an integral part of this meal and should be served both as a sauce for the pork and as a dip for the artichokes. Tapénade can be made in advance and refrigerated for up to two weeks.

WHAT TO DRINK

It is difficult to choose a wine to accompany artichokes, but the other dishes in this menu go well with a full-bodied white wine or a relatively light red. For the white, try a white Châteauneuf-du-Pape or a Mâcon; for the red, Italian Valpolicella or Bardolino.

SHOPPING LIST AND STAPLES

2½- to 2¾-pound pork loin, boned, rolled, and tied
4 medium-size globe artichokes
12 to 14 cloves garlic
Small bunch fresh oregano, or 1 teaspoon dried
Small bunch fresh sage, or 1 tablespoon dried
Small bunch fresh basil
4 lemons
2-ounce can anchovy fillets
10-ounce jar oil-cured black olives
⅔ cup plus 2 tablespoons olive oil
3½-ounce jar capers
1 loaf French bread
Salt and freshly ground black pepper

UTENSILS

Barbecue grill with cover
Mesquite for barbecuing, if available
Food processor or blender
Large saucepan with cover
Roasting pan with rack, if not using barbecue
Colander
Strainer
Measuring cups and spoons
Chef's knife

Paring knife
Slotted spoon
Rubber spatula
Juicer
Instant-reading meat thermometer
Rake for barbecue
Heatproof mitt
Kitchen towel

START-TO-FINISH STEPS

Thirty minutes ahead: If using barbecue, start fire, using mesquite, if available.

1. Follow pork recipe steps 1 through 6.
2. While pork is cooking, follow artichoke recipe steps 1 through 4.
3. While artichokes are cooking, follow tapénade recipe step 1.
4. Follow artichokes recipe steps 5 and 6.
5. While artichokes are cooling, follow pork recipe step 7.
6. Follow pork recipe step 8.
7. Follow tapénade recipe steps 2 through 3 and artichokes recipe step 7. Slice bread and place in basket.
8. Follow pork recipe step 9 and serve with artichokes, tapénade, and bread.

RECIPES

Pork Loin Roasted with Garlic and Sage

1 lemon
2½- to 2¾-pound pork loin, boned, rolled, and tied
Salt and freshly ground black pepper
5 fresh sage leaves, or 1 tablespoon dried rubbed sage, plus sage sprigs for garnish (optional)
4 cloves garlic
Tapénade (see following recipe)

1. If not using barbecue, preheat oven to 475 degrees.
2. Halve lemon. Squeeze one half over pork and rub meat with juice.
3. Sprinkle pork with salt and pepper to taste and with dried sage, if using, and pat lightly to make grains adhere.
4. Peel and sliver garlic. Arrange garlic on top of pork in 2 lengthwise rows. If using fresh sage, wash, pat dry with paper towels, and place end to end, between rows of garlic.
5. If barbecuing, move coals with barbecue rake to one side, leaving space in center. Place grill 4 inches from coals and heat 2 to 3 minutes.
6. If barbecuing, place pork in center of grill, not over coals. Cover barbecue, open vents in lid, and cook pork 50 to 60 minutes, or until instant-reading meat thermometer registers 155 degrees. If not barbecuing, lay pork on rack in roasting pan and place in oven. Cook 10 minutes, lower oven temperature to 375 degrees, and cook 40 to 50 minutes more, or until instant-reading meat thermometer registers 155 degrees.
7. Slice remaining lemon half for garnish, if desired.

8. Remove pork from barbecue or oven and, if serving warm, let rest 10 minutes.
9. When ready to serve, cut pork into ½- to ¾-inch-thick slices. Arrange slices on platter, garnish with lemon slices and sage sprigs, if desired, and serve with tapénade.

Artichokes Oreganata

4 medium-size globe artichokes
2 branches fresh oregano, or 1 teaspoon dried
1 lemon
4 cloves garlic
2 tablespoons olive oil
2 teaspoons salt
Basil sprigs for garnish (optional)
Tapénade (see following recipe)

1. In large covered saucepan, bring 2 quarts water to a boil over high heat.
2. Carefully spreading leaves apart, wash artichokes thoroughly under cold running water. Drain, and with very sharp paring knife, trim stems and prickly ends of leaves.
3. If using fresh oregano, remove stems and wash. With chef's knife, halve lemon and unpeeled garlic cloves. Add one lemon half, garlic, fresh or dried oregano, olive oil, and salt to boiling water.
4. Add artichokes to boiling water. Moisten folded clean kitchen towel and place on top of artichokes, cover saucepan, reduce heat, and simmer until point of knife easily penetrates base of artichoke, about 25 minutes.
5. With slotted spoon, transfer artichokes to colander and set upside down to drain. Let sit at least 20 minutes.
6. Slice remaining lemon half and, if using basil sprigs for garnish, wash and pat dry.
7. Arrange artichokes on platter, garnish with lemon slices and basil sprigs, if desired, and serve with tapénade.

Tapénade

½-pound oil-cured black olives
3 tablespoons capers
6 anchovy fillets
Small bunch fresh basil
4 to 6 cloves garlic, approximately
2 lemons
⅔-cup olive oil
1 loaf French bread

1. With paring knife, pit olives. In strainer, rinse capers and anchovies, drain, and pat dry with paper towels. In colander, wash basil and pat dry with paper towels. Remove stems and discard. With chef's knife, coarsely chop enough leaves to measure ½ cup. Peel garlic and juice lemons.
2. In bowl of food processor or blender, combine olive oil, olives, capers, anchovies, basil, garlic, and lemon juice. Purée mixture until it is thick and smooth.
3. Using rubber spatula, transfer tapénade to sauce bowl. Garnish with basil sprig, if desired, and serve with bread.

Bruce Cliborne

MENU 1 (Left)
Mesquite-Grilled Clams, Oysters, and Lobsters
Herbed New Potatoes, Carrots, and Scallions
Cucumbers and Tomatoes with Lime

MENU 2
Grilled Loin of Pork with Fresh Thyme
Marinated Corn Salad
Sweet-and-Sour Peaches and Plums

MENU 3
Sea Scallops with Herbed Crème Fraîche
Poached Fennel
Orange, Radish, and Coriander Salad

Bruce Cliborne's clambake captures the essence of out-of-doors entertaining. For his Menu 1, prepare the meal on the beach to enjoy the scent of the sea mingling with the grilling oysters, clams, and lobsters—an experience at once both primitive and sophisticated. Traditional beach clambakes, devised by the early New England Indians, call for steaming an assortment of shellfish in a bed of seaweed over hot stones. For his version, Bruce Cliborne cooks both seafood and foil-wrapped vegetables over a mesquite fire. Of course, the grilled seafood is just as delicious prepared in your backyard.

Menus 2 and 3, both sumptuous picnics, are ideal for backyards or terraces but are easily transportable to some away-from-home site. Bruce Cliborne intends the fragrant thyme that scents the pork loin of Menu 2 to evoke images of flower-filled meadows. Menu 3 consists of poached scallops on a wreath of radicchio leaves, braised fennel, and a delicately seasoned orange and radish salad.

All three menus combine seasonal choices with abundant contrasting textures, colors, and flavors. This approach to meal planning is in keeping with Bruce Cliborne's art training. As art students learn classic techniques, he believes, so cooks should master the skills of fine chefs: "Making good food should be challenging, intriguing, amusing, and hard work," he says.

Grilled clams, oysters, and lobsters—a variation of the traditional New England clambake—constitute an impressive main course for this barbecue. Arrange the potatoes, carrots, and scallions on a serving platter, and serve the cucumber and tomato salad in a separate bowl. Each guest will need a ramekin of saffron-butter sauce for dunking the shellfish.

Mesquite-Grilled Clams, Oysters, and Lobsters
Herbed New Potatoes, Carrots, and Scallions
Cucumbers and Tomatoes with Lime

For Bruce Cliborne's clambake, the lobsters, clams, and oysters are grilled over mesquite (for information on mesquite, see page 11). You can bring your own portable barbecue or, as the cook recommends, construct a pit grill at the beach, but this requires some advance preparation. For a pit grill, use the rack from your own barbecue or construct one at home: Make a grill rack by nailing four 2 foot x 2 inch x 1-inch pieces of wood together. Over this frame, stretch ¼-inch heavy-duty mesh wire and, with a staple gun, staple it to the frame at each corner. For the fire, dig a shallow sand pit 1 foot deep and slightly less than 2 feet square. Lay the mesquite in the pit, and ignite it by using crumpled paper, kindling, or firestarter. Once the fire has started, lay the mesh frame over the pit. Of course, if you do not live near a beach, you may prepare this clambake over a barbecue in your own backyard.

WHAT TO DRINK

The lobster deserves a first-rate dry white wine with full flavor and body. Try a Chardonnay from California, a good white Burgundy from a named village, or a white Mercurey.

SHOPPING LIST AND STAPLES

2 medium-size live lobsters (about 1¼ pounds each), with claws pegged or bound
12 clams
12 oysters
16 small new potatoes (about 2 pounds total weight)
12 baby finger carrots (about ½ pound total weight)
3 medium-size tomatoes, or 6 Italian plum tomatoes (about ¾ pound total weight)
4 medium-size cucumbers (about 2 pounds total weight)
2 large shallots
1 bunch scallions, or 18 pearl onions
2 cloves garlic
Small bunch fresh chives
Small bunch fresh basil
Small bunch fresh sage, rosemary, or thyme
2 small limes
2 sticks unsalted butter
¾ cup virgin olive oil
2 tablespoons white wine vinegar or tarragon vinegar
Pinch of saffron threads

Salt and freshly ground pepper
1 cup dry white wine

UTENSILS

2-foot-square grilling rack from barbecue (optional)
Mesquite for barbecue, if available
Small saucepan
2 large bowls
Small bowl
Colander
Sieve
Measuring cups and spoons
Chef's knife
Paring knife
Oyster knife
Slotted spoon
Wooden spoon
Teaspoon
Metal spatula (optional)
Juicer
Tongs
Vegetable peeler
Wire scrubbing brush
Nutcracker

START-TO-FINISH STEPS

1. Start barbecue, using mesquite, if available.
2. Follow potatoes recipe steps 1 through 4.
3. Follow cucumbers recipe steps 1 through 5.
4. Follow clams recipe steps 1 through 3.
5. Follow potatoes recipe step 5.
6. Follow clams recipe steps 4 through 8.
7. Follow potatoes recipe step 6.
8. Follow clams recipe steps 9 through 12 and potatoes recipe step 7.
9. Follow cucumbers recipe step 6, potatoes recipe step 8, clams recipe step 13, and serve.

RECIPES

Mesquite-Grilled Clams, Oysters, and Lobsters

12 clams
12 oysters

2 large shallots
2 medium-size live lobsters (about 1¼ pound each), with
    claws pegged or bound
1 cup dry white wine
6 leaves fresh basil, chopped
Pinch of saffron threads
2 sticks unsalted butter
Salt and freshly ground pepper

1. With wire brush, scrub clams and oysters thoroughly, and rinse in several changes of cold water.
2. Peel shallots and chop enough to measure 1 tablespoon.
3. Set sieve over small saucepan. Using oyster knife, open oysters over sieve, and pour liquor through sieve into pan. Loosen oysters from shell bottoms and discard bottoms. On aluminum foil, set aside oysters in half shells.
4. To kill lobsters, place them belly-up with claws still pegged or bound. While gripping lobster securely through folded towel with one hand, sever spinal cord with the other by plunging tip of knife crosswise into lobster at point where body section and tail section meet (involuntary muscle spasms may continue after lobster is dead).

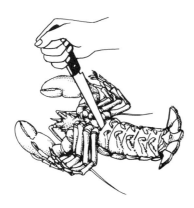

5. When fire is ready, place lobsters on grill set 8 inches from heat and cook 7 to 8 minutes.
6. For sauce, bring oyster liquor to a boil over high heat. Add wine and shallots, and reduce, stirring occasionally, until about 3 tablespoons remain, about 15 minutes.
7. While sauce is reducing, chop basil.
8. Grill oysters and clams until edges of oysters have curled and clams have opened, 10 to 12 minutes.
9. Turn lobsters and cook until bright red, 4 to 7 minutes.
10. Rub saffron threads between thumb and forefinger and add to sauce. Reduce heat to low.
11. Cut butter into 1-tablespoon pieces. Add butter to sauce, 1 tablespoon at a time, stirring until thoroughly incorporated. Add salt and pepper to taste.
12. Transfer lobsters, oysters, and clams to serving trays or platter and crack lobsters with nutcracker.
13. Add basil to saffron-butter sauce and divide sauce among individual ramekins. Serve sauce alongside shellfish.

Herbed New Potatoes, Carrots, and Scallions

16 small new potatoes (about 2 pounds total weight)
12 baby finger carrots (about ½ pound total weight)

9 scallions, or 18 pearl onions
½ cup virgin olive oil
1 tablespoon minced fresh sage, rosemary, or thyme

1. In colander, rinse and drain potatoes, carrots, and scallions. Pat dry with paper towels.
2. With vegetable peeler, peel carrots. Trim scallions, removing roots and all but 2 inches of green, or peel onions, if using.
3. In large bowl, combine carrots, scallions, and potatoes. Drizzle with olive oil and toss until evenly coated. Sprinkle with sage, rosemary, or thyme and toss again.
4. Cut four 12-inch squares of aluminum foil and divide carrots and potatoes evenly among them. With slotted spoon, transfer carrots and potatoes to lower half of foil, arranging them in a single layer. Fold down top half of square, being careful not to disturb vegetables, and crimp edges of foil to seal. Reserve remaining oil in bowl.
5. Place packets on grill and cook 15 minutes without turning.
6. With tongs or metal spatula, carefully remove packets from grill. Open packets and add scallions or onions next to, not on top of, carrots and potatoes. If desired, add remaining oil from bowl. Reseal packets and return to grill, turning packets so "uncooked" side is down. Cook 15 minutes.
7. Remove packets from grill and leave sealed until ready to serve.
8. Open packets and turn vegetables into serving bowl.

Cucumbers and Tomatoes with Lime

3 medium-size tomatoes or 6 Italian plum tomatoes
    (about ¾ pound total weight)
4 medium-size cucumbers (about 2 pounds total weight)
2 cloves garlic
2 small limes
¼ cup virgin olive oil
2 tablespoons white wine vinegar or tarragon vinegar
1 tablespoon chopped fresh chives
1 tablespoon chopped fresh basil, plus additional sprigs
    for garnish (optional)
Salt and freshly ground pepper

1. Wash tomatoes and pat dry with paper towels. With chef's knife, cut tomatoes into ¼-inch-thick slices. Transfer to large bowl.
2. With vegetable peeler, peel cucumbers. Halve cucumbers lengthwise and, with teaspoon, scoop out seeds and discard.
3. Lay cucumbers cut side down and slice into ¼-inch-thick crescents. Add to bowl with tomatoes.
4. Peel and mince garlic. Squeeze enough lime juice to measure ¼ cup.
5. In small bowl, combine garlic, lime juice, olive oil, vinegar, chives, basil, and salt and pepper to taste. Beat with fork until blended.
6. Pour dressing over salad and toss gently until evenly coated. Garnish with basil sprigs, if desired.

Grilled Loin of Pork with Fresh Thyme
Marinated Corn Salad
Sweet-and-Sour Peaches and Plums

For this elegant picnic, serve the pork and vegetables at room temperature, and the fruit cooled.

Grill the slices of pork loin in a cast-iron grilling pan, a versatile piece of equipment that cooks meat and fish quickly with relatively little oil or fat. These pans, which resemble corrugated or ridged frying pans, sit directly on the flame. For this recipe, brush the ridged surface with olive oil, then lay sprigs of fresh thyme on the ridges before adding the pork slices. If you do not own this kind of pan, use a heavy-gauge skillet instead.

A napkin-lined wicker basket is attractive as well as convenient for serving the sliced grilled pork loin. Large glass jars with tight-fitting lids are perfect for carrying and serving the poached fruit and the marinated salad.

Thyme is a highly aromatic woody perennial that grows relatively easily in sunny garden plots. Its tiny leaves contain various powerful oils that make them pungent and flavorful even when dried. Fresh thyme may be available from specialty food stores or from certain greengrocers.

For the last course, peaches and plums are poached in wine and balsamic vinegar, a mellow, slightly sweet, aged Italian vinegar. When the fruit is cooked, remove it immediately from the poaching liquid to preserve its texture.

WHAT TO DRINK

The best choice here would be beer or ale. If you prefer wine, pick a soft fruity white: a German or California Riesling, or a California French Colombard.

SHOPPING LIST AND STAPLES

Four 1¾-inch-thick center-cut pork loin slices, boned and trimmed (about 1½ pounds total weight)
2 medium-size red bell peppers
4 ears fresh corn, or two 10-ounce packages frozen kernels
6 large shallots (about ¼ pound total weight)
1 clove garlic
Small bunch parsley
Small bunch thyme
2 medium-size lemons
Medium-size orange
4 large barely ripe peaches
8 large firm plums
4 Anjou or Bosc pears (if peaches or plums are unavailable)
¼ cup plus 3 tablespoons virgin olive oil
1 tablespoon balsamic vinegar or red wine vinegar
2 tablespoons sherry vinegar or red wine vinegar
15-ounce package golden raisins
⅓ cup brown sugar
2 whole cloves
Salt and freshly ground pepper
½ teaspoon black peppercorns
3 tablespoons dry white wine
2 cups red wine, preferably Burgundy

UTENSILS

Large saucepan with cover
Large sauté pan
Large cast-iron grilling pan or cast-iron skillet
2 large bowls
Small bowl or jar
Platter
Colander
Measuring cups and spoons
Chef's knife
Paring knife
2 slotted spoons
Wooden spoon
Metal spatula
Tongs
Zester (optional)
Vegetable peeler
Juicer
2 large jars with lids or other carrying containers

START-TO-FINISH STEPS

1. Follow peaches recipe steps 1 through 6. While liquid is simmering, chill platter for peaches.
2. Follow peaches recipe step 7.

3. While fruit is poaching, peel shallots and follow corn recipe steps 1 through 3.
4. Follow peaches recipe step 8.
5. Follow corn recipe steps 4 through 10.
6. Follow pork recipe steps 1 through 5.
7. Follow corn recipe step 11, peaches recipe step 9, and pork recipe step 6.

RECIPES

Grilled Loin of Pork with Fresh Thyme

3 tablespoons olive oil, approximately
12 sprigs thyme
Four 1¾-inch-thick center-cut pork loin slices, boned and
    trimmed (about 1½ pounds total weight)
Salt
Freshly ground pepper

1. Coat bottom of grill pan with oil.
2. Heat pan over medium-high heat. Add 4 thyme sprigs. When thyme releases its fragrance, add pork slices, arranging them in single layer.
3. Reduce heat to medium-low and cook pork 12 to 15 minutes. Using tongs, remove thyme sprigs as they char and replace them with fresh sprigs. If using cast-iron pan, pour off pork fat as it accumulates.
4. Using tongs, turn pork and cook until slightly browned and running juices show no trace of pink, 12 to 15 minutes. Season with salt and pepper to taste.
5. With metal spatula or tongs, transfer pork to paper towels to drain. Let cool 10 minutes.
6. Pack in foil for transporting.

Marinated Corn Salad

¼ cup virgin olive oil
6 large shallots (about ¼ pound total weight), peeled
2 medium-size red bell peppers
1 clove garlic
½ teaspoon black peppercorns
Salt
Freshly ground pepper
4 ears fresh corn, or two 10-ounce packages frozen
    kernels
½ teaspoon fresh thyme
1½ teaspoons coarsely chopped parsley
3 tablespoons dry white wine
2 teaspoons sherry vinegar or red wine vinegar

1. In large sauté pan, heat 2 tablespoons olive oil over medium heat 30 seconds. Reduce heat to low, add shallots, and cook, stirring frequently with wooden spoon, until translucent and crisp-tender, 4 to 5 minutes.
2. Wash red peppers and pat dry with paper towels. Halve, core, and seed peppers. Cut each half lengthwise into 3 sections. Peel and mince garlic. Crush peppercorns.
3. With slotted spoon, transfer shallots to large bowl.
4. Add red peppers to sauté pan and season with salt and pepper to taste. Cook in remaining oil over medium-low heat stirring frequently with wooden spoon, until peppers are just barely tender, about 10 minutes.
5. If using fresh corn, trim stub end so that it will rest flat on cutting board. Holding corn perpendicular to cutting board, slice downward with chef's knife, removing kernels. Turn ear and repeat until all kernels are removed.
6. With slotted spoon, transfer cooked peppers to bowl with shallots.
7. Add corn to sauté pan and cook, stirring frequently, until corn is tender, about 6 minutes.
8. Add garlic and crushed black peppercorns to corn and stir to combine.
9. With slotted spoon, transfer corn to bowl with shallots and peppers. Add thyme, parsley, white wine, and vinegar and stir to combine.
10. Let mixture cool to room temperature, stirring frequently.
11. Pack cooled mixture into jar with tight-fitting lid or other suitable container.

Sweet-and-Sour Peaches and Plums

Medium-size orange
2 medium-size lemons
4 large barely ripe peaches
8 large firm plums
4 Anjou or Bosc pears (if peaches or plums are
    unavailable)
½ cup golden raisins
⅓ cup firmly packed brown sugar
1 tablespoon balsamic vinegar or red wine vinegar
2 whole cloves
2 cups red wine, preferably Burgundy

1. In large saucepan, bring 2½ quarts water to a boil over high heat.
2. Fill large bowl with ice water. Strip zest from ½ orange and cut zest into ⅛-inch julienne strips. Juice lemons.

3. Add peaches and plums, or pears, if using, to boiling water and blanch about 30 seconds.

4. With slotted spoon, gently but rapidly transfer fruit to bowl of ice water and let sit 1 minute. Transfer fruit to colander and drain.

5. With paring knife or fingers, peel fruit, being careful not to pierce flesh.

6. In saucepan, combine raisins, lemon juice, brown sugar, vinegar, orange zest, cloves, and red wine. Bring to a simmer over medium-high heat, and cook 5 minutes.

7. Add fruit and simmer gently, removing each piece of fruit when barely tender, 3 to 6 minutes for plums, 4 to 8 minutes for peaches, and 13 to 18 minutes for pears, if using.

8. With slotted spoon, transfer fruit to chilled platter and transfer poaching syrup to chilled small bowl or jar with metal spoon in it to absorb heat. Let cool to room temperature, 30 to 45 minutes. Refrigerate, if desired.

9. When ready to leave for picnic, recombine fruit and syrup in jar with tight-fitting lid or other suitable container.

ADDED TOUCH

The artichokes are filled with a savory stuffing of prosciutto (an Italian ham) and either wild or shiitake mushrooms. Fresh cultivated mushrooms will also do.

Artichokes Stuffed with Wild Mushrooms and Prosciutto

Salt
4 medium-size to large artichokes
3 medium-size lemons
½ pound thinly sliced prosciutto
½ pound wild Black Forest, shiitake, or golden oak mushrooms, preferably, or fresh cultivated mushrooms
2 medium-size red bell peppers
¾ cup olive oil
½ teaspoon chopped thyme
½ teaspoon chopped oregano
3 cloves garlic
¼ cup red wine vinegar
½ teaspoon chopped parsley
Freshly ground pepper

1. In large saucepan, bring 3½ quarts water and 4 teaspoons salt to a boil over high heat.

2. Holding artichokes under cold running water, gently force leaves apart and rinse thoroughly. Trim off stems and any wilted or browned leaves.

3. Add artichokes to boiling water and reduce to a simmer. Juice lemons and add juice and rinds to pan. Fold a clean dishcloth in half, wet it, and place directly on top of artichokes to keep them moist as they float to surface.

4. Cook artichokes at a simmer just until point of knife easily penetrates base and leaves pull off with little resistance, 30 to 45 minutes.

5. Fill large bowl with ice water. With slotted spoon, rapidly transfer artichokes to ice water. Leave 1 minute and transfer to colander.

6. When cool enough to handle, part center leaves of each artichoke with your fingers. Using teaspoon, if necessary, remove innermost leaves and center spikes just above the heart. Set artichokes upside down on paper towels to drain.

7. With chef's knife, slice prosciutto into ¼-inch julienne strips. Wipe mushrooms with damp paper towels and cut into ¼-inch-thick slices. Wash peppers and pat dry with paper towels. Halve, core, and seed peppers. Cut each half into ¼-inch-thick strips.

8. In medium-size skillet, heat 2 tablespoons olive oil over medium heat about 30 seconds. Add prosciutto and sauté, stirring frequently with wooden spoon, until strips stiffen and crisp slightly, 3 to 4 minutes. Drizzle in more olive oil, if necessary, to prevent sticking. With slotted spoon, transfer prosciutto to large bowl.

9. Add 2 tablespoons olive oil to skillet and heat 30 seconds. Add mushrooms and sauté, stirring frequently, until mushrooms are lightly browned, 7 to 10 minutes. With slotted spoon, transfer mushrooms to bowl.

10. Add 2 tablespoons olive oil to skillet and heat 30 seconds. Add red pepper strips and sauté over medium heat until crisp-tender, about 4 minutes. With slotted spoon, transfer peppers to bowl.

11. Add thyme and oregano to prosciutto mixture and toss to combine.

12. Turn artichokes right side up. With teaspoon, stuff center of artichokes with equal amounts of mixture and set aside.

13. Peel and mince garlic.

14. In medium-size jar with tight-fitting lid, combine remaining olive oil, vinegar, garlic, parsley, and pepper to taste. Shake dressing until blended and spoon over each artichoke just before serving.

Sea Scallops with Herbed Crème Fraîche
Poached Fennel
Orange, Radish, and Coriander Salad

Serve the sliced sea scallops on a bed of radicchio leaves and garnish them with mint. The poached fennel or celery and the orange-red salad require individual bowls. If you wish, offer a basket of fresh bread with the meal.

Prepare this picnic far enough in advance to allow all its components to chill thoroughly.

Sea scallops, unlike the smaller bay scallops, are available fresh most of the year and are sold frozen as well. For this menu, scallops are served with *crème fraîche*, a French cultured-cream product resembling sour cream. Not many supermarkets stock *crème fraîche*, but you can easily make your own in advance.

WHAT TO DRINK

Try an Alsatian or California Gewürztraminer to complement the spiciness of the menu.

SHOPPING LIST AND STAPLES

1½ pounds sea scallops
4 fennel bulbs (about 2¼ pounds total weight) or
 4 hearts of celery
2 heads radicchio or Boston lettuce
2 medium-size carrots
Small bunch radishes (6 to 8)
Large red onion
Medium-size Spanish onion
1 clove garlic
Small bunch thyme or rosemary (optional)
Small bunch parsley
Small bunch mint
Small bunch basil
8 medium-size seedless oranges
1 lemon
1 cup crème fraîche, homemade or commercial
2 cups chicken stock, preferably homemade (see page 13),
 or canned
½ cup virgin olive oil
⅓ cup red wine vinegar or tarragon vinegar
4 bay leaves
3 star anise
1 tablespoon coriander seeds
1 teaspoon green peppercorns
1 teaspoon Szechwan peppercorns or black peppercorns
Salt and freshly ground pepper
2 cups dry white wine

UTENSILS

Large stainless steel or enamel-lined skillet with cover
Medium-size stainless steel sauté pan

Platter
Large bowl
Medium-size bowl
Small bowl
Salad spinner (optional)
Sieve
Measuring cups and spoons
Chef's knife
Paring knife
Slotted spoon
Wooden spoon
Grater
Vegetable peeler
Zester (optional)
3 large carrying containers with lids (if packing up picnic)

START-TO-FINISH STEPS

1. Follow fennel recipe steps 1 through 3.
2. While fennel is poaching, follow scallops recipe steps 1 through 4.
3. Follow salad recipe step 1.
4. Follow fennel recipe step 4 and scallops recipe steps 5 through 9.
5. Follow salad recipe steps 2 and 3, and scallops recipe step 10.
6. Follow scallops recipe step 11 and salad recipe step 4.
7. Follow scallops recipe step 12, salad recipe step 5, fennel recipe step 5, and serve or pack up picnic.

RECIPES

Sea Scallops with Herbed Crème Fraîche

Medium-size Spanish onion
2 medium-size carrots
1 lemon
3 star anise
1 teaspoon green peppercorns
2 bay leaves
2 heads radicchio or Boston lettuce
1 cup dry white wine
1½ pounds sea scallops
1 cup crème fraîche, well chilled
1 tablespoon chopped mint
1 tablespoon chopped basil
Salt

1. Peel onion and carrots, and cut into ⅛-inch-thick slices.
2. Strip zest from lemon.
3. In stainless steel skillet, combine 2 cups cold water, onion, carrots, lemon zest, star anise, green peppercorns, and bay leaves. Cover, bring to a boil over medium-high heat, and simmer, partially covered, 20 minutes.
4. Wash radicchio and dry in salad spinner or pat dry with paper towels. Set platter in refrigerator to chill.
5. Add wine to poaching liquid and simmer 5 minutes.
6. Wipe scallops with damp paper towels. With chef's knife, halve each scallop.

7. Pour poaching liquid through sieve set over large bowl. Return sieved liquid to skillet and return to a simmer over medium-high heat. Rinse out bowl.
8. Add scallops and poach 2 to 3 minutes.
9. With slotted spoon, transfer scallops to chilled platter and refrigerate 10 minutes.
10. In cleaned bowl, combine crème fraîche and herbs.
11. Add chilled scallops to crème fraîche mixture, and toss gently to combine. Add salt to taste and toss again.
12. In large carrying container with lid or in serving dish, arrange radicchio or lettuce leaves in a wreath. Spoon scallops into center of wreath.

Poached Fennel

1 clove garlic, peeled and minced
2 cups chicken stock
1 cup dry white wine
2 bay leaves
Salt and freshly ground pepper
4 fennel bulbs or 4 hearts of celery
1 tablespoon chopped parsley

1. In medium-size stainless steel sauté pan, combine garlic, stock, wine, bay leaves, and salt and pepper to taste. Bring to a boil over medium-high heat.
2. With chef's knife, trim fennel, leaving about 6 inches of stalk, and remove nubbin at bottom of bulb. Rinse bulb under cold water and pat dry with paper towels. Quarter bulb lengthwise.
3. Add fennel to pan, lower heat, and simmer until barely tender when pierced with knife, 20 to 30 minutes.
4. With slotted spoon, transfer fennel to serving platter or to carrying container and cool at least 20 minutes.
5. Before serving or packing, sprinkle fennel or celery with parsley.

Orange, Radish, and Coriander Salad

8 medium-size seedless oranges
Large red onion, peeled and sliced
Small bunch radishes (6 to 8), washed and trimmed
½ cup virgin olive oil
⅓ cup red wine vinegar or tarragon vinegar
1 teaspoon Szechwan peppercorns or black peppercorns
1 tablespoon coriander seeds
Salt and freshly ground pepper

1. With paring knife, trim peel and white pith from oranges. Then, over medium-size bowl or deep carrying container with lid, holding orange in one hand and knife in other, free segments by cutting toward center on each side of membranes, letting segments fall into bowl.
2. Separate onion into rings and add to oranges.
3. Coarsely grate radishes into bowl with orange mixture. Using wooden spoon, toss gently to combine.
4. In small bowl, combine oil, vinegar, peppercorns, coriander seeds, and salt and pepper to taste.
5. Pour dressing over salad and toss gently but thoroughly until salad is well-coated with dressing.

Nicholas Baxter

MENU 1 (Right)
**Loin of Lamb with Tomato
and Mushroom Stuffing
Watercress and Hazelnut Salad
Orzo with Sour Cream and Black Pepper**

MENU 2
**Grilled Salmon Steaks with Fresh Dill and Thyme
Mélange of Fresh Vegetables**

MENU 3
**Loin of Veal Poached with Vegetables
in White Wine
Wild Rice with Red Pepper and Cassis**

Nicholas Baxter has a straightforward culinary maxim: A glorious meal does not require a multitude of ingredients and lengthy preparation. Quality components, carefully arranged on the dinner plate, will please both the palate and the eye. "If the meal does not form an alluring still life on the plate," he says, "guests do not quickly discover that it tastes good."

When he plans a meal, he makes one course spectacular and downplays the rest. This way, the diners' taste buds are not overwhelmed. For Menu 1, the focal point is barbecued lamb, a delicious alternative to grilled beef. Stuffed with a flavorful chopped tomato mixture, which provides a textural contrast, the lamb is served with a watercress and hazelnut salad, and orzo with sour cream.

The grilled salmon steaks in Menu 2 are the centerpiece, accompanied by mixed spring vegetables. The loin of veal in Menu 3 is poached in a stock based on Alsatian Riesling, which the chef calls the nearest thing to fresh grapes in wine form.

Garnish the barbecued loin of lamb with lettuce leaves and tomato wedges, and serve it on a platter. Sprinkle the orzo with fresh snipped chives. The watercress salad is easy to carry in a covered serving dish.

Loin of Lamb with Tomato and Mushroom Stuffing
Watercress and Hazelnut Salad
Orzo with Sour Cream and Black Pepper

Cook this backyard barbecue in stages: Complete the salad and orzo indoors in the intervals between basting the lamb outdoors.

The loin, the tenderest cut of lamb, is filled with a tomato and mushroom stuffing and then tied up with string. Ask your butcher to bone the loin and to cut an envelope for the stuffing between the top layer of fat and the meat. You can oven-roast the lamb, but it tastes best barbecued.

Watercress is available at most supermarkets and greengrocers year round. The leaves should be crisp and green and have no sign of wilt or discoloration. Rinse watercress in cold water, pat it dry with paper towels, and refrigerate the bunch in a plastic bag, where it will keep for a week. If you wish, you can use dandelion greens or arugula instead. Hazelnuts, sometimes known as filberts, are slightly sweet and less oily than pecans. They are sold in bulk at specialty food shops and many health food stores. If not available, you can use slivered almonds instead.

WHAT TO DRINK

Grilled lamb with garlic calls for a dry red wine; try a California Cabernet Sauvignon, a claret from the Médoc, or a Bordeaux village wine, such as a St. Julien or Margaux.

SHOPPING LIST AND STAPLES

3 pounds loin of lamb, boned, with pocket cut lengthwise between fat and meat
4 medium-size tomatoes plus 1 large tomato (optional)
6 ounces mushrooms
Small head Boston lettuce (optional)
3 bunches watercress, or 2 bunches dandelion greens (about 1 pound total weight)
Small bunch fresh chives
Large Spanish onion
2 cloves garlic
1 lemon
½ pint sour cream
2 tablespoons unsalted butter
16-ounce can tomato purée
¼ cup plus 2 tablespoons extra-virgin olive oil
16-ounce box orzo
¼ pound shelled hazelnuts, preferably, or 4-ounce can slivered almonds

1 tablespoon dried oregano
Salt and freshly ground black pepper

UTENSILS

Barbecue
Food processor (optional)
Medium-size skillet
Medium-size saucepan
Small saucepan
18-inch jelly-roll pan
Medium-size bowl
Small bowl
Salad bowl
Colander
Salad spinner (optional)
Measuring cups and spoons
Chef's knife
Carving knife
Paring knife
Slotted spoon
2 wooden spoons
2 metal spatulas or 2 barbecue forks
Carving board
Juicer (optional)
Basting brush
Garlic press
Kitchen string

START-TO-FINISH STEPS

Thirty minutes ahead: Start barbecue and place rack 4 inches from coals.

1. Follow stuffing recipe steps 1 through 7.
2. Follow lamb recipe steps 1 through 8.
3. While lamb is cooking, follow orzo recipe step 1.
4. While water is heating, follow lamb recipe step 9.
5. Follow orzo recipe step 2.
6. While orzo is cooking, follow salad recipe steps 1 through 3.
7. Follow orzo recipe steps 3 and salad recipe step 4.
8. Follow orzo recipe steps 4 and 5.
9. Follow lamb recipe step 10.
10. While meat is resting, follow orzo recipe step 6 and salad recipe step 5.
11. Carve lamb and serve with salad and orzo.

Loin of Lamb with Tomato and Mushroom Stuffing

2 cloves garlic
3 pounds loin of lamb, boned, with pocket cut lengthwise
    between fat and surface of meat
Tomato and Mushroom Stuffing (see following recipe)
¼ cup extra-virgin olive oil
1 tablespoon dried oregano
Small head Boston lettuce for garnish (optional)
Large tomato for garnish (optional)

1. Peel garlic and cut in half lengthwise.
2. With cut side of garlic, rub inside of lamb pocket, both fat and meat.
3. With garlic press, crush garlic into tomato and mushroom stuffing and stir to combine.
4. With slotted spoon, scoop up stuffing mixture, allowing each spoonful to drain slightly, and fill lamb pocket.
5. Using kitchen string, carefully tie up lamb to close the pocket, securing the stuffing inside.
6. In small bowl, combine olive oil and oregano.
7. When fire is ready, place lamb on grill 4 inches above coals. Using basting brush, brush lamb with oil mixture.
8. When flames from the dripping fat have subsided, lower rack to within 3 inches of coals. Cook lamb, turning and basting every 8 to 10 minutes, until juices run pale pink, a total of about 40 minutes.
9. For garnish, if using, wash lettuce and dry in salad spinner or pat dry with paper towels. Wash tomato, if using, pat dry, and cut into wedges.
10. Just before meat is done, line serving platter with lettuce leaves, if using. With 2 metal spatulas or 2 barbecue forks, transfer meat to platter. Carefully remove string, and let lamb rest 5 to 10 minutes before carving.

Tomato and Mushroom Stuffing

4 medium-size tomatoes
Large Spanish onion
6 ounces mushrooms
¼ cup tomato purée
2 tablespoons unsalted butter
½ tablespoon salt

1. In small saucepan, bring just enough water to cover tomatoes by ½ inch to a boil over high heat.
2. While water is heating, with paring knife cut a cross in the top and bottom of each tomato, just penetrating skin. Peel onion and set aside. Wipe mushrooms with damp paper towels and, using paring knife, trim off ¼ inch of stems. Quarter mushrooms lengthwise, or, if very large, cut into eighths.
3. When water is boiling, add tomatoes and blanch 30 seconds. In colander, drain tomatoes and cool under cold running water. Peel off skins.
4. Halve, seed, and core tomatoes. Cut each half into ½-inch dice and place in medium-size bowl. Add tomato purée and, using wooden spoon, stir to combine. Add mushrooms and mix well.
5. In food processor, chop onion coarsely, pulsing on and off about 6 seconds. Or, with chef's knife, chop coarsely.
6. In medium-size skillet, heat butter over medium heat until just melted, about 1 minute. Do not let butter brown. Add onion to skillet and cook over medium heat, stirring occasionally with wooden spoon, 3 minutes.
7. Add tomato and mushroom mixture, and stir to combine. Season with salt, and cook over medium heat about 5 minutes, or until mixture has thickened slightly. Remove pan from heat and set aside.

Watercress and Hazelnut Salad

3 bunches watercress or 2 bunches dandelion greens
    (about 1 pound total weight)
1 cup shelled hazelnuts, preferably, or ½ cup slivered almonds
1 lemon
2 tablespoons extra-virgin olive oil
Salt and freshly ground black pepper

1. Preheat oven to 350 degrees.
2. Wash watercress or dandelion greens and dry in salad spinner or pat dry with paper towels. Remove stems from watercress or trim dandelion stems and discard. Place greens in salad bowl, cover with plastic wrap and refrigerate until ready to serve.
3. Place hazelnuts on jelly-roll pan and toast in oven 4 to 6 minutes. If using almonds, toast 3 to 4 minutes, or until very lightly browned.
4. Remove hazelnuts from oven and allow to cool slightly. Juice lemon and strain to remove pits.
5. Spoon olive oil over watercress or dandelion greens and toss until evenly coated. Add lemon juice and toss again. Sprinkle salad with nuts and season with salt and pepper to taste.

Orzo with Sour Cream and Black Pepper

½ pound orzo
Small bunch fresh chives
3 tablespoons sour cream
2 teaspoons salt
Freshly ground black pepper

1. In medium-size saucepan, bring 8 cups of water to a boil over high heat.
2. Add orzo to boiling water and simmer until tender, 9 to 10 minutes.
3. In colander, drain orzo and allow to cool, tossing occasionally with wooden spoon.
4. Wash chives, pat dry with paper towels, and chop enough to measure 2 tablespoons.
5. When orzo is cool, transfer to medium-size bowl. Add sour cream and, using 2 wooden spoons, toss until evenly coated. Add salt and toss again.
6. Just before serving, grind black pepper to taste over orzo and sprinkle with chives.

Grilled Salmon Steaks with Fresh Dill and Thyme
Mélange of Fresh Vegetables

On individual trays, arrange the salmon garnished with dill and lemon slices and the vegetables, all in foil wrappings.

For this simple barbecue, grill both components of the meal, wrapped in foil packets, simultaneously. As the meal's focal point, Nicholas Baxter has selected salmon steaks, whose firm texture makes them ideal for grilling. The vegetable packets consist of leeks, tomatoes, and zucchini. Be sure to wash the leeks carefully (see page 43); sand gets trapped in the leafy tops.

WHAT TO DRINK

To stand alongside the rich flavor of the fish, choose either a California Sauvignon Blanc or a French Pouilly Fumé.

SHOPPING LIST AND STAPLES

4 salmon steaks (each about 8 ounces)
8 small leeks
8 medium-size tomatoes
4 medium-size zucchini, each about 6 inches long
Medium-size bunch fresh dill, or 1 tablespoon dried
Medium-size bunch fresh thyme, or 1 tablespoon dried
Small bunch fresh basil, or 2 tablespoons dried
2 lemons, plus additional lemon (optional)
4 tablespoons unsalted butter

½ cup sweet apple cider
Salt and freshly ground pepper

UTENSILS

Barbecue
Large saucepan
Colander
Measuring cups and spoons
Chef's knife
Paring knife
Zester (optional)
Heatproof mitt

START-TO-FINISH STEPS

1. Start barbecue.
2. If using fresh herbs, strip thyme leaves from branches. Wash dill and basil, and pat dry with paper towels. With chef's knife, chop basil separately and then chop dill and thyme.
3. Follow vegetables recipe steps 1 through 6.
4. Follow salmon recipe steps 1 through 4.
5. When vegetables have been on grill 5 minutes, follow salmon recipe step 5.
6. Follow salmon recipe step 6, and vegetables recipe step 7, and serve.

RECIPES

Grilled Salmon Steaks with Fresh Dill and Thyme

2 lemons, plus additional lemon for garnish (optional)
4 salmon steaks (each about 8 ounces)
3 tablespoons chopped fresh dill, or 1 tablespoon dried
3 tablespoons chopped fresh thyme, or 1 tablespoon
  dried, plus 4 branches for garnish (optional)
4 tablespoons unsalted butter
Salt and freshly ground pepper

1. Slice 1 lemon into wedges for garnish, if desired. Grate zest from 2 lemons.
2. With damp paper towels, wipe salmon steaks. Sprinkle both sides of steaks with dill, thyme, and lemon zest.
3. Cut four 12-inch-square sheets of foil and place 1 salmon steak on lower half of each. Top each steak with 1 tablespoon butter.
4. Bring free half of foil over steak to form rectangle. Fold edges together and crimp to seal.
5. When grill is ready, place packets on barbecue and cook 5 minutes. Turn and cook 5 minutes on other side.
6. Transfer packets to individual basket, if desired. Open packets, season with salt and pepper to taste, and garnish with lemon wedges and a branch of thyme, if desired.

Mélange of Fresh Vegetables

8 small leeks
4 medium-size zucchini, each about 6 inches long

8 medium-size tomatoes
¼ cup chopped fresh basil, or 2 tablespoons dried
½ cup sweet apple cider
Salt and freshly ground pepper

1. In large saucepan, bring to a boil enough water to cover tomatoes by about 1 inch.
2. With chef's knife, trim greens and roots from leeks, and discard. Split leeks lengthwise and rinse thoroughly under cold running water to remove sand and grit.
3. Trim ends from zucchini, wash, and pat dry. With chef's knife, quarter each zucchini lengthwise.
4. Plunge tomatoes into boiling water and blanch 30 seconds. Transfer tomatoes to colander and refresh under cold running water. Peel, quarter, and seed tomatoes.
5. Cut four 12-inch-square sheets of aluminum foil. Divide vegetables equally among sheets. Sprinkle each portion with basil and 2 tablespoons cider. Fold edges of foil together and crimp to seal.
6. Place packets on barbecue and cook 15 minutes.
7. To serve, unwrap packets and season with salt and pepper to taste.

ADDED TOUCH

Potato starch makes this cake light and airy. If unavailable, substitute white flour in the same proportion.

Light Chocolate Cake

½ cup potato starch (potato flour)
⅔ cup Dutch cocoa powder
6 eggs
½ cup sugar
½ cup milk

1. Preheat oven to 325 degrees.
2. Sift together potato starch and cocoa powder.
3. Separate eggs, placing yolks in small bowl and whites in large bowl.
4. Using electric mixer, beat yolks until thick and lemon-colored, about 5 minutes. Yolks should form a continuous ribbon from raised beater. Wash and dry beaters thoroughly.
5. Beat egg whites at slow speed until they foam, 2 to 3 minutes. Increase speed to medium and beat whites until they form soft peaks, about 3 minutes. Sprinkle in sugar, increase speed to high, and beat until whites are stiff but still shiny.
6. Reduce speed to low and gradually pour in yolks. When yolks are almost completely incorporated, sprinkle in cocoa powder mixture, add milk all at once, and beat just until blended.
7. Turn batter into ungreased 9 x 5 x 2½-inch loaf pan.
8. Place pan on middle rack of oven and bake until cake tester inserted in center comes out clean, 50 to 60 minutes.
9. Remove pan from oven and place, upside down, so it is supported at ends by 2 heatproof items of same height. Let pan hang 10 minutes.
10. Turn cake onto rack and let cool.

Loin of Veal Poached with Vegetables in White Wine
Wild Rice with Red Pepper and Cassis

This picnic consists of sliced loin of veal served with celery and carrots and accompanied by wild rice and red pepper strips.

Plan this menu as a backyard picnic so you can serve the meal slightly warm. If you wish to have an away-from-home picnic, wrap each dish—first in foil, then in a layer of newspaper—to keep the meal warm until serving.

The main-dish loin of veal is poached in a broth made from chicken stock and Riesling wine. Produced in the Alsace region, Riesling is a perfect partner for delicately flavored meats. It is dry, fruity, and fresh-tasting.

To make the savory sauce for the veal, reduce the poaching liquid over high heat to half its original volume and add the caraway seeds to it before you set it aside to cool.

Wild rice is not a rice at all but the seeds of a wild grass.

Because it is always in short supply, it is expensive, but in this recipe half a pound serves four people. Before cooking, wild rice needs thorough rinsing to remove the excessively smoky taste. Deep burgundy-colored *crème de cassis*, a French black currant liqueur, is stirred thoroughly into the wild rice and thinly coats the grains.

WHAT TO DRINK

The veal dish calls for something completely dry and rather full-bodied. Try a California Chardonnay or a relatively simple white Burgundy, like a Mâcon or St. Véran.

2½ pounds center-cut veal tenderloin, boned, rolled, and tied
8 baby carrots
1 bunch celery
Large red bell pepper
4 pearl onions
4 cups chicken stock, preferably homemade (see page 13), or canned
½ pound wild rice
½ teaspoon caraway seeds
2 bay leaves
Salt
Freshly ground black pepper
14 black peppercorns
1 bottle Alsatian Riesling
¼ cup crème de cassis

UTENSILS

2 medium-size saucepans, with covers
Large heavy-gauge shallow casserole
Large bowl
2 medium-size bowls
Sieve
Measuring cups and spoons
Chef's knife
Carving knife
Paring knife
Slotted spoon
2 wooden spoons
Double-pronged fork
Vegetable peeler
Meat thermometer
Corkscrew

START-TO-FINISH STEPS

1. Follow veal recipe steps 1 and 2.
2. While stock is heating, follow rice recipe steps 1 and 2.
3. While water is coming to a boil, follow veal recipe step 3.
4. Follow rice recipe step 3.
5. While rice is cooking, follow veal recipe step 4.
6. Follow rice recipe step 4 and veal recipe steps 5 and 6.
7. Follow rice recipe step 5 and veal recipe step 7.
8. Follow rice recipe step 6, veal recipe steps 8 and 9, and serve.

RECIPES

Loin of Veal Poached with Vegetables in White Wine

4 stalks celery
4 pearl onions
8 baby carrots
1 bottle Alsatian Riesling
4 cups chicken stock

14 black peppercorns
2 bay leaves
2½ pounds center-cut veal tenderloin, boned, rolled, and tied
½ teaspoon caraway seeds
Salt
Freshly ground pepper

1. With chef's knife, trim celery stalks, halve, and cut into 4-inch strips. Peel onions and scrape carrots. Set aside.
2. In large casserole, combine wine, stock, peppercorns, bay leaves, and onions. Add veal and enough water to cover. With wooden spoon, stir liquid and seasonings, and bring to a simmer over high heat.
3. Lower heat to maintain a very gentle simmer, cover partially, and cook 20 minutes.
4. Add celery and carrots, partially cover pan, and continue to simmer until meat thermometer placed in center of veal registers 150 degrees, about 10 minutes.
5. With double-pronged fork and slotted spoon, transfer veal and vegetables to medium-size bowl. Discard onions and bay leaves. Add 2 cups cooking liquid to bowl with veal and vegetables, and leave uncovered to cool, 15 to 20 minutes.
6. For sauce, transfer remaining cooking liquid to large bowl. To reduce liquid quickly, measure 2½ cups back into casserole and 2½ cups into medium-size saucepan. Bring both to a boil over high heat and reduce each to ¾ cup, about 15 minutes. Stir ¼ teaspoon caraway seeds into each pan and set both aside to cool, about 10 minutes.
7. Stir reduced cooking liquid in casserole into reduced liquid in saucepan and season to taste with salt and pepper.
8. With slotted spoon, transfer veal to carving board. Remove string and slice veal into ¼-inch-thick medallions.
9. Place a few tablespoons of sauce on each plate and top with veal medallions. With slotted spoon, remove vegetables from liquid and arrange alongside veal. Serve remaining sauce separately.

Wild Rice with Red Pepper and Cassis

½ pound wild rice
Large red bell pepper
¼ cup crème de cassis

1. In sieve, rinse rice thoroughly under cold running water.
2. In medium-size saucepan, bring 4 cups water to rapid boil over high heat.
3. Add rice to boiling water and, with wooden spoon, stir once. Reduce to a simmer, cover, and cook until tender but still slightly *al dente*, 40 minutes.
4. Wash red pepper and pat dry with paper towels. With chef's knife, halve, core, and seed pepper. Slice into ¼-inch-thick strips.
5. Drain rice in sieve and let stand 10 minutes, tossing gently with fork every 2 or 3 minutes.
6. While rice is still warm, transfer to medium-size bowl. Add peppers and cassis, and stir gently to combine.

Frank Bailey

MENU 1 (Left)
Spinach Pâté
Pasta Salad with Pesto
Cold Orange Duck

MENU 2
Chilled Cream of Tomato Soup with Tequila
Fajitas
Spanish Rice Salad

MENU 3
Grilled Shrimp with Butter Sauce
Grilled Baked Fish
Roasted Pepper Salad

Frank Bailey, a native Texan, always chooses what his local markets carry rather than buy food imported from other regions or from overseas. For instance, a Dover sole flown in from England is never as good as sea trout caught locally the same day. He advises novice cooks to use whatever is the freshest, even if that means departing from a recipe. "Food is more a product of place than of people," he explains. "Creole cooking, for example, never tastes quite the same outside of New Orleans."

This self-taught cook says his recipes are interpretations of Creole and Cajun cooking, cuisines founded on French techniques and embellished by many other ethnic influences. Sophisticated Creole cooking features well-seasoned yet subtle seafood and vegetable dishes. Cajun cooking, its country cousin, is more pungent and peppery. He uses these same basic ingredients, but he tones down his meals by using herbs rather than hot spices like Cayenne or hot pepper sauces. Menu 3 features two dishes—grilled fish and grilled shrimp—served often in New Orleans, but here they are seasoned with butter and herbs.

Menu 1 is an elegant picnic of baked duck breasts, served cold with a zesty orange juice, mustard, and herb dressing. A spinach pâté and a pasta salad flavored with pesto accompany the duck.

Menu 2 reflects Frank Bailey's Texas heritage. He features *fajitas* (Spanish for "little strips"), a Sunday-afternoon barbecue dish from southern Texas. After grilling, the meat is sliced and wrapped in flour tortillas with chopped avocado to make a sandwich. The rest of the meal consists of a chilled tomato soup spiked with tequila and a Spanish rice salad.

For this picnic, arrange the spinach pâté, partially sliced, on a serving platter. Garnish the duck breasts with parsley and a curl of orange zest, and mound the pasta salad in its own bowl. Fill a picnic basket with bread for easy serving.

Spinach Pâté
Pasta Salad with Pesto
Cold Orange Duck

Because a pâté is so easy to carry, it is perfect picnic fare. In this recipe, for which a food processor is essential, chicken breasts and fresh spinach are puréed and then baked in a spinach-lined mold.

Fresh or frozen duck breasts are available in meat markets and some supermarkets. To thaw duck breasts, place them, still wrapped, in the refrigerator for a day.

The dressing for the pasta salad is a variation on the classic Italian pesto sauce; instead of pine nuts, the cook substitutes shelled pecans for a stronger nut flavor.

All three dishes in this menu should be prepared ahead of time and chilled.

WHAT TO DRINK

A young, medium-bodied red wine would be a perfect complement to this duck recipe.

SHOPPING LIST AND STAPLES

1 pound boned chicken breasts
4 boned duck breasts (about 6 ounces each)
2 pounds spinach
Small red bell pepper (optional)
Medium-size carrot
Medium-size onion
2 shallots
4 cloves garlic
1 large or 2 medium-size bunches fresh basil
Small bunch fresh tarragon, or 1 teaspoon dried
Small bunch fresh thyme, or ½ teaspoon dried
Small bunch fresh parsley (optional)
1 lemon
Small orange
4 eggs
1 pint heavy cream
2 tablespoons unsalted butter
¼ pound Pecorino Romano or Parmesan cheese
1½ cups extra-virgin olive oil
2 tablespoons red wine vinegar
2 tablespoons whole-grain mustard, preferably Creole
1 pound pasta shells, preferably fresh
2¾-ounce bag shelled pecans
¼ teaspoon nutmeg
¼ teaspoon Cayenne pepper (optional)
1 tablespoon arrowroot
Salt and freshly ground pepper
¼ cup dry red wine

UTENSILS

Food processor
Large saucepan with cover
13 x 9-inch metal baking pan
8½ x 4¼ 3-inch loaf pan or straight-sided mold
2 platters
Large bowl
2 small bowls
Colander
Sieve
Salad spinner (optional)
Measuring cups and spoons
Chef's knife
Paring knife
Large cooking spoon
Wooden spoon
Metal spatula
Whisk
Grater
Juicer (optional)
Vegetable peeler

START-TO-FINISH STEPS

1. Follow pâté recipe steps 1 through 13.
2. While pâté is cooking, follow duck recipe steps 1 through 4.
3. While duck is cooking, follow pasta recipe steps 1 through 6.
4. Follow duck recipe steps 5 through 10.
5. Follow pâté recipe step 14.
6. Follow duck recipe step 11, pâté recipe steps 15 and 16, and pack duck, pâté, and pasta for picnic, if desired.

RECIPES
Spinach Pâté

4 eggs
1 shallot
2 cloves garlic
2 pounds spinach
1 pound boned chicken breasts
1 tablespoon arrowroot
1½ cups heavy cream
¼ teaspoon nutmeg
Salt and freshly ground pepper

1 teaspoon chopped fresh tarragon, or ½ teaspoon dried
¼ teaspoon Cayenne pepper (optional)
2 tablespoons unsalted butter
Small red bell pepper for garnish (optional)

1. Using 2 small bowls, separate eggs, reserving yolks for another use. Peel shallot and garlic.
2. In large covered saucepan, bring 3 quarts water to a boil over high heat.
3. Wash spinach thoroughly under cold running water and remove tough stems. Set aside 8 leaves for garnish, if desired.
4. Plunge spinach into boiling water and blanch 30 seconds. In colander, drain immediately and refresh under cold water.
5. Spread half of spinach over paper-towel-lined platter. Using additional paper towels, blot spinach as dry as possible.
6. With your hands, squeeze remaining spinach until it no longer exudes any liquid.
7. Preheat oven to 375 degrees.
8. Coarsely dice chicken. In bowl of food processor, combine chicken with squeezed spinach, shallots, and garlic. Pulse until mixture becomes a paste, 15 seconds. Add 1 tablespoon arrowroot and pulse once.
9. Add egg whites to mixture and process 30 seconds. Slowly drizzle in cream and process until blended.
10. Add nutmeg and salt and pepper to taste, and stir to combine. Add tarragon and Cayenne, if using, and stir.
11. Butter loaf pan or straight-sided mold and line bottom and sides with two-thirds of blanched spinach leaves. Spoon chicken-spinach mixture into pan, smooth surface, and cover with blanched spinach. Cover pan with foil.
12. Bake until firm, about 45 minutes.
13. Wash red pepper, if using for garnish, and pat dry with paper towels. Halve, core, and seed pepper. Cut pepper into strips. If desired, make a bed of reserved unblanched spinach on serving platter.
14. Remove pâté from oven, discard foil, and let rest 5 minutes.
15. To unmold, with your thumbs, pull edge of pan away from pâté, and, holding platter against pan, invert pan and platter. The pâté should slide out onto the platter. If it sticks, still holding pan and platter together, give a sharp downward jerk.
16. Serve pâté warm or cold, garnished with red pepper strips, if using.

Pasta Salad with Pesto

Salt
2 cups fresh basil leaves, plus sprigs for garnish (optional)
1 pound pasta shells, preferably fresh
¼ pound Pecorino Romano or Parmesan cheese
2 cloves garlic, peeled
½ cup shelled pecans
¾ cup extra-virgin olive oil
Freshly ground pepper

1. In large covered saucepan, bring 2 quarts water with 4 teaspoons salt to a boil over high heat.
2. While water is heating, stem basil, wash leaves, and dry in salad spinner or pat dry with paper towels.
3. Add pasta to pan and cook according to package directions until just *al dente*.
4. While pasta is cooking, prepare sauce: Using food processor, grate enough cheese to measure ½ cup. Add garlic, basil, and pecans to cheese in food processor bowl and pulse until puréed. With processor running, slowly drizzle in all but 2 tablespoons oil. Season purée with salt and pepper to taste.
5. In colander, drain pasta thoroughly. Off heat, return shells to pan and toss with remaining oil.
6. Add sauce to warm pasta and toss gently to combine. Transfer to serving bowl and let cool. Serve garnished with basil sprigs, if desired.

Cold Orange Duck

Small orange
Medium-size onion
1 shallot
Medium-size carrot
4 boned duck breasts (about 6 ounces each)
¼ cup dry red wine
2 tablespoons whole-grain mustard, preferably Creole
2 tablespoons red wine vinegar
¾ cup extra-virgin olive oil
1 teaspoon chopped fresh thyme, or ½ teaspoon dried
1 teaspoon chopped fresh tarragon, or ½ teaspoon dried
Salt and freshly ground pepper
Parsley sprigs for garnish (optional)

1. Grate enough orange zest to measure 1 tablespoon and squeeze enough juice to measure 1 tablespoon. Cut strips of zest for garnish, if desired.
2. Peel onion and shallot and chop coarsely. Peel carrot and chop coarsely. Place onion, shallot, and carrot in metal baking pan.
3. Pierce duck skin several times with tines of fork and set duck on top of vegetables.
4. Place baking pan in oven and bake duck 20 minutes.
5. Transfer duck to platter and let cool.
6. Using large spoon, skim off fat from juices in pan.
7. Over medium heat, deglaze pan by adding red wine and stirring vigorously with wooden spoon, scraping up any browned bits clinging to bottom of pan.
8. Raise heat to medium-high and reduce liquid to about 2 tablespoons, 2 to 3 minutes.
9. In large bowl, combine reduced liquid, mustard, and vinegar, and whisk until thoroughly blended. Slowly drizzle in oil, whisking constantly, until mixture is thick and smooth, 3 to 5 minutes.
10. With whisk, beat in orange zest and juice, thyme, tarragon, and pepper to taste. Pour sauce over duck and stir gently to combine.
11. Serve garnished with parsley sprigs and strips of zest, if desired.

Chilled Cream of Tomato Soup with Tequila
Fajitas
Spanish Rice Salad

For this hearty barbecue, offer the sliced skirt steak with avocado chunks, the rice salad, and the tomato soup in plastic containers. Serve the flour tortillas folded attractively in a napkin-lined basket.

Skirt steak is the traditional cut of meat for this Texas barbecue, but you may substitute flank steak. Before grilling, the meat marinates in vermouth, melted butter, minced garlic, and fresh chopped coriander, an herb that looks like parsley but has a more pungent taste.

Softened flour tortillas are used to make the Mexican-style sliced-steak sandwiches. These tortillas are available at well-stocked supermarkets.

WHAT TO DRINK

The flavors and spices of this menu call for either beer or ale or a slightly chilled light red wine such as a Spanish Rioja or a Beaujolais.

SHOPPING LIST AND STAPLES

2 pounds beef skirt steak, ¼ to ½ inch thick, or flank steak
½ cup fresh peas or 10-ounce package frozen
2 large avocados
1 medium-size onion
Small bunch fresh parsley
Small bunch fresh coriander
Small bunch fresh basil, or 2 tablespoons dried
4 to 5 cloves garlic
3 limes
½ pint heavy cream
½ pint sour cream
2 tablespoons unsalted butter
½ cup chicken stock, preferably homemade (see page 13), or canned
28-ounce can Italian plum tomatoes
24-ounce can mixed tomato-vegetable juice
¾ cup plus 2 tablespoons olive oil, approximately
2 tablespoons red wine vinegar or sherry wine vinegar
8 flour tortillas, fresh or frozen
½ cup rice
1 teaspoon Cayenne pepper
½ teaspoon curry powder
Salt and freshly ground pepper
½ cup dry vermouth
2 tablespoons sweet vermouth
¼ cup tequila

UTENSILS

Barbecue
Food processor or blender
Large saucepan with cover
Medium-size saucepan with cover
Small saucepan
13 × 9 × 2-inch glass or stainless steel baking dish
Measuring cups and spoons
Chef's knife
Paring knife
Wooden spoon
Barbecue tongs
Fork
2 carrying containers

START-TO-FINISH STEPS

1. Follow soup recipe steps 1 and 2.
2. Follow fajitas recipe steps 1 and 2.
3. Start barbecue.
4. Follow soup recipe steps 3 and 4.
5. If using fresh peas for rice recipe, wash and drain. If using frozen peas, measure ½ cup and set out to thaw. Follow rice recipe steps 1 through 3.
6. Follow fajitas recipe steps 3 and 4.
7. Follow rice recipe steps 4 and 5, and fajitas recipe step 5.
8. While fajitas are grilling, follow soup recipe step 5 and serve.
9. Follow fajitas recipe steps 6 through 8 and serve with rice salad.

RECIPES

Chilled Cream of Tomato Soup with Tequila

2 tablespoons olive oil
2 cloves garlic, peeled and minced
2 cups drained canned Italian plum tomatoes
½ cup dry vermouth
¼ cup fresh basil leaves, or 2 tablespoons dried, plus
   1 tablespoon chopped fresh basil for garnish (optional)
2 cups mixed tomato-vegetable juice, chilled
¼ cup heavy cream
¼ cup sour cream
¼ cup tequila
½ teaspoon curry powder
Salt and freshly ground pepper

1. In large saucepan, heat oil over medium heat. Add garlic and cook, stirring, until translucent, 2 to 3 minutes.
2. Stir in tomatoes and vermouth, and cook 15 minutes, covered, over medium heat.
3. In food processor or blender, combine tomato mixture and basil, and purée. Add juice, heavy cream, and sour cream, and process until blended.
4. Add tequila, curry powder, and salt and pepper to taste, and process briefly to combine. Cover and chill at least 30 minutes.
5. Serve garnished with fresh chopped basil, if desired.

Fajitas

2 tablespoons unsalted butter
2 to 3 cloves garlic, peeled and minced
2 tablespoons sweet vermouth
2 tablespoons chopped fresh coriander
2 pounds beef skirt steak, ¼ to ½ inch thick,
   or flank steak
2 large avocados
¼ cup lime juice plus 1 lime, quartered, for garnish
Salt and freshly ground pepper
8 flour tortillas

1. In small saucepan, melt butter over low heat. Add garlic and sauté 1 minute. Remove pan from heat, add vermouth and coriander, and stir to combine.
2. Place meat in baking dish and, using your fingers, coat both sides of meat with vermouth mixture.
3. Peel and halve avocados lengthwise. Remove and discard pit. Cut avocados into 1½-inch chunks and place in carrying container. Toss avocado gently with lime juice. Add salt and pepper to taste and toss again.
4. Separate tortillas into 2 piles and wrap in foil.
5. Place meat on grill rack set 4 inches from heat and cook until outside of meat has browned, about 4 minutes per side for skirt steak and 6 to 8 minutes per side for flank steak. Place tortilla packets on side of grill to warm.
6. To make fajitas, cut meat widthwise across grain into ¼-inch-thick strips. If using flank steak, cut steak in half lengthwise and then slice each half as for skirt steak.
7. Add fajitas to avocado and toss to combine.
8. Serve fajitas with flour tortillas and lime wedges.

Spanish Rice Salad

½ to ¾ cup olive oil
1 medium-size onion, peeled and chopped
½ cup rice
1 cup drained canned Italian plum tomatoes
½ cup chicken stock
1 teaspoon Cayenne pepper
1 tablespoon chopped fresh parsley
¼ teaspoon cumin
½ cup peas
Salt and freshly ground pepper
2 tablespoons red wine vinegar or sherry wine vinegar

1. In medium-size saucepan, heat ¼ cup olive oil over medium heat. Add onion and cook, stirring frequently, until lightly browned, about 5 minutes.
2. Add rice and cook, stirring, 3 minutes, or until rice appears slightly translucent.
3. Stir in tomatoes and stock. Bring to a boil over medium-high heat, stirring occasionally to prevent sticking. Reduce heat, stir in remaining ingredients, but omit frozen peas, if using. Simmer, covered, 18 minutes.
4. Remove pan from heat, add thawed frozen peas, if using, and turn rice into carrying container.
5. With fork, fluff rice. Add vinegar and remaining ¼ to ½ cup olive oil, and toss gently to combine.

Grilled Shrimp with Butter Sauce
Grilled Baked Fish
Roasted Pepper Salad

Serve the grilled shrimp in their shells for a decorative touch. The main-dish fish has its own parsley and dill seasoning as a garnish. Arrange overlapping pieces of tomatoes and red peppers on lettuce leaves for the salad.

For this backyard barbecue menu, both the shrimp appetizer and the fish entrée cook on the grill. The shrimp cook in their shells, which keep them from sticking to the grill and drying out. Let your guests remove the shells as they eat, by pulling off the legs and peeling off the shell along the underside.

WHAT TO DRINK

The fresh, bright flavors of this menu are complemented by a dry, crisp white wine. First choice would be a French Muscadet, second an Italian Verdicchio.

SHOPPING LIST AND STAPLES

1½ to 2 pounds large unshelled shrimp, heads removed
Four ¾-inch-thick fillets of red snapper, Pacific ocean perch, or another firm white-fleshed fish (each about 6 ounces)
3 small red bell peppers (about ¾ pound total weight)
Small head Boston lettuce
¼ pound snow peas or tiny green beans
2 medium-size tomatoes (about 1 pound total weight)
2 shallots
Small bunch scallions
2 cloves garlic
Medium-size bunch rosemary, or 1 tablespoon dried
Small bunch fresh dill, or 1 teaspoon dried
Small bunch fresh parsley
Medium-size bunch fresh tarragon or oregano, or 1 teaspoon dried
2 lemons
1 egg
1 stick plus 2 tablespoons unsalted butter
2 tablespoons tarragon vinegar or wine vinegar
½ cup extra-virgin olive oil
2½ tablespoons whole-grain sharp mustard, preferably Creole
1 bay leaf
1 teaspoon whole peppercorns
Salt and freshly ground pepper
½ cup beer

UTENSILS

Barbecue
2 small saucepans

2 medium-size bowls, one glass or stainless steel
Platter
Colander
Salad spinner (optional)
Measuring cups and spoons
Chef's knife
Paring knife
Wooden spoon
Metal spatula
Whisk
Tongs
Paper bag

START-TO-FINISH STEPS

1. Start barbecue.
2. Follow pepper salad recipe steps 1 through 11.
3. Follow shrimp recipe steps 1 through 5 and fish recipe steps 1 and 2.
4. Follow shrimp recipe steps 6 through 8.
5. Follow fish recipe steps 3 and 4 and serve with pepper salad.

RECIPES

Grilled Shrimp with Butter Sauce

2 cloves garlic
1 teaspoon whole peppercorns
1 stick unsalted butter
½ cup beer
2 tablespoons whole-grain sharp mustard, preferably Creole
1½ to 2 pounds large unshelled shrimp, heads removed
¼ cup fresh rosemary, or 1 tablespoon dried
1 bay leaf
Salt
Parsley sprigs for garnish (optional)

1. Peel and crush garlic. Crush peppercorns.
2. In small saucepan, melt butter over low heat.
3. In medium-size glass bowl, whisk together beer and mustard.
4. Whisking constantly, drizzle in butter until thoroughly incorporated.
5. Add shrimp, rosemary, bay leaf, peppercorns, and salt to taste, and, with wooden spoon, stir to coat shrimp.
6. Set grill rack 4 inches from coals. When coals are ready, using tongs lay shrimp on grill, and cook until they have become orange, 2 to 3 minutes per side. (Timing will depend on size of shrimp.)
7. Return shrimp to bowl, and toss to coat with sauce.
8. Serve warm or hot, garnished with parsley sprigs, if desired, and let your guests shell the shrimp as they eat.

Grilled Baked Fish

2 tablespoons butter, at room temperature
2 shallots, peeled and chopped
2 lemons

Four ¾-inch-thick fillets of red snapper, Pacific ocean perch, or another firm white-fleshed fish (each about 6 ounces)
1 tablespoon chopped fresh dill, or 1 teaspoon dried
1 tablespoon chopped fresh parsley
Salt and freshly ground pepper

1. Cut four 12-inch-square sheets of aluminum foil and butter 8-inch-square center section of each.
2. Thinly slice lemons and place 2 slices in center of each foil square. Lay fish on top of lemon and sprinkle each fillet with shallots, dill, parsley, and salt and pepper to taste. Fold over aluminum foil and crimp edges to seal.
3. Place packets on grill 4 inches from heat and grill just until fish flakes easily with tip of sharp knife, about 6 minutes.
4. Open packets and, using spatula, transfer fish to platter. Garnish with remaining lemon slices, if desired.

Roasted Pepper Salad

3 small red bell peppers (about ¾ pound total weight)
Small head Boston lettuce
2 scallions
2 medium-size tomatoes (about 1 pound total weight)
¼ pound snow peas, or tiny green beans
1 egg
2 tablespoons tarragon vinegar or wine vinegar
½ teaspoon Creole mustard
¼ cup minced tarragon or oregano, loosely packed, or 1 teaspoon dried
½ cup extra-virgin olive oil
Salt and freshly ground pepper

1. Preheat broiler and place broiler tray 4 inches from heat.
2. Wash peppers and pat dry with paper towels.
3. Place peppers on broiler tray and broil, turning as needed, until entire skin is charred, 3 to 4 minutes.
4. While peppers are broiling, bring 1 quart water to a boil in small saucepan.
5. Using metal spatula, transfer peppers to paper bag. Roll up bag and leave peppers to sweat, 15 minutes.
6. Wash lettuce and dry in salad spinner or pat dry with paper towels. Wash, pat dry, trim, and chop scallions. Wash tomatoes, pat dry, and cut into ½-inch-thick slices.
7. String snow peas or beans, and blanch in boiling water, 2 minutes. Drain in colander and refresh under cold running water.
8. Separate egg, placing yolk in medium-size bowl, and reserving white for another use. To egg yolk, add scallions, vinegar, mustard, and tarragon or oregano, whisking until smooth.
9. Gradually drizzle in oil, whisking constantly, until mixture is thick and smooth. Add salt and pepper to taste.
10. Remove peppers from bag and peel away charred skin. Halve, seed, and core peppers. Cut peppers into ½-inch strips.
11. Line platter with lettuce and arrange tomatoes, snow peas, and peppers on top. Pour dressing over salad.

John Risser

MENU 1 (Right)
Marinated Chicken Breasts
Potato Salad Vichyssoise
Mushroom and Cauliflower Salad

MENU 2
Barbecued Beef Kabobs
Tomatoes with Goat Cheese
Cucumber and Grapefruit Salad

MENU 3
Grilled Stuffed Lamb Chops
Mixed Bean Salad
Cheese and Fruit Medallions

When John Risser plans a meal, he considers such variables as the weather, the season, the hour, and the available ingredients. "Food should always suit the occasion," he says. For such special-occasion meals as picnics and barbecues, he selects components for their enticing aromas, strong flavors, and basic simplicity. His recipes often reflect his love for provincial French and country-style Italian foods. Menus 2 and 3 best exemplify these preferences. The fragrant seasoning for the kabobs of Menu 2, redolent with rosemary, garlic, orange zest, olive oil, and shallots, has its roots in French Provençal cooking. His use of Oriental sesame oil is a departure from classical French seasonings, and it enhances the rich flavor of the grilled beef. The tomato and goat cheese salad, and the cucumber-grapefruit salad are Italian-style dishes. For Menu 3, he pairs grilled lamb with a medley of fresh beans, a provincial French combination. The fruit and cheese course is typically European.

The chicken breasts of Menu 1, marinated in a lemony mixture of his own devising, are a break from his French and Italian bonds. The accompanying potato salad Vichyssoise tastes like the potato and leek soup for which it is named, but, in the salad, chives replace leeks.

A colorful setting for this barbecue highlights the grilled chicken breasts, served on a platter and garnished with basil or parsley and lemon slices. Arrange the two salads in informal serving pieces.

Marinated Chicken Breasts
Potato Salad Vichyssoise
Mushroom and Cauliflower Salad

For this barbecue, make the two salads ahead of time so they cool thoroughly, and cook the chicken as the last step. The grilled chicken breasts, flavored with a lemon juice marinade, make a festive main course. You will need boneless breasts, skin on, which are readily available from your butcher. The skin protects the delicate chicken during grilling.

For the potato salad Vichyssoise, dressed with both sour cream and mayonnaise, use baking potatoes. Their slightly grainy texture contrasts with the creamy dressing.

For the second salad, blanch the cauliflower pieces briefly to soften them, then refresh them in cold water. This instantly stops further cooking. A cauliflower head should be creamy white and firm. Avoid those with loose or open flower clusters and with yellow spots. Refrigerate the cauliflower wrapped in perforated plastic. It will keep up to four days. The secret of perfect salad mushrooms is to buy them very fresh, firm and unblemished. The caps should fit tightly over the stems with no gills showing. You can store mushrooms briefly in the refrigerator in a container covered with a damp paper towel. Never wash mushrooms: to clean them, wipe them off with a damp paper towel.

WHAT TO DRINK

This is definitely a white-wine menu. Choose a Riesling from Germany, Washington, or New York, or try an Italian Pinot Bianco or Pinot Grigio.

SHOPPING LIST AND STAPLES

4 whole boneless chicken breasts, unskinned (about 2 pounds total weight)
6 to 8 small baking potatoes (2 to 3 pounds total weight)
Small head cauliflower (1 to 1½ pounds)
½ pound mushrooms
2 bunches celery
Medium-size onion
1 clove garlic
1 fresh chili pepper (optional)
Large bunch fresh chives
Small bunch fresh thyme, or ½ teaspoon dried
Small bunch fresh basil, or 1 teaspoon dried
Small bunch fresh parsley (optional)
2 lemons, plus one additional (optional)

½ pint sour cream
½ cup mayonnaise
1 cup olive oil
¼ cup tarragon wine vinegar
Salt
Freshly ground black pepper
Freshly ground white pepper

UTENSILS

Barbecue
Large saucepan with cover
Medium-size saucepan with cover
Small heavy-gauge saucepan
13 × 9 × 2-inch glass or stainless steel baking dish
Salad bowl
Large bowl
Small bowl
Colander
Measuring cups and spoons
Chef's knife
Paring knife
2 wooden spoons
Grater
Juicer
Basting brush
Tongs
Vegetable peeler
Dish towel
Thin rubber gloves (optional)

START-TO-FINISH STEPS

1. Follow potato salad recipe steps 1 through 4.
2. While potatoes are cooking, start barbecue.
3. Follow potato salad recipe step 5.
4. While potatoes are drying out, follow chicken recipe steps 1 through 4.
5. While chicken marinates, follow potato salad recipe steps 6 and 7.
6. Follow cauliflower recipe steps 1 through 6.
7. Follow potato salad recipe step 8.
8. Follow chicken recipe steps 5 and 6.
9. Five minutes before chicken is done, follow potato salad recipe steps 9 and 10, and cauliflower recipe steps 7 and 8.
10. Follow chicken recipe step 7, and serve with potato salad and cauliflower salad.

RECIPES

Marinated Chicken Breasts

Medium-size onion
Large clove garlic
2 lemons, plus one for garnish (optional)
½ cup olive oil
2 sprigs fresh thyme, or ½ teaspoon dried
2 tablespoons chopped fresh basil, or 1 teaspoon dried,
    plus 4 sprigs basil or parsley for garnish (optional)
1 teaspoon salt
½ teaspoon freshly ground black pepper
4 whole boneless chicken breasts, unskinned (about 2
    pounds total weight)

1. Peel onion and garlic. With chef's knife, cut onion into ⅛-inch-thick slices and separate into rings. Mince garlic. Set aside.
2. Squeeze enough lemon juice to measure ½ cup. Grate enough lemon zest to measure 1 tablespoon. Slice remaining lemon for garnish, if desired.
3. In shallow glass or stainless steel baking pan, combine onion, garlic, lemon juice, zest, olive oil, thyme, basil, salt, and pepper. With wooden spoon, stir to combine.
4. Add chicken breasts and turn to coat with marinade. Leave breasts, skin side up, so cut side sits in marinade. Seal dish with plastic wrap and marinate chicken at least 30 minutes.
5. When barbecue is ready, place grill rack 3 inches from heat source. Arrange chicken breasts on rack, cut side down, and grill 1 minute. With tongs, turn breasts and grill 1 minute more.
6. Raise grill rack to 4 inches. Transfer marinade to small heavy-gauge saucepan. Set pan on side of grill and bring marinade to a simmer. Brush chicken with marinade and continue cooking and basting until chicken is firm to the touch, about 15 minutes. Turn chicken as needed to ensure even color.
7. With tongs, transfer chicken breasts to plate. If desired, garnish with lemon slices, sprigs of basil or parsley, and onion rings from the marinade.

Potato Salad Vichyssoise

Salt
6 to 8 small baking potatoes (2 to 3 pounds total weight)
½ cup mayonnaise
½ cup sour cream
¼ cup chopped fresh chives plus 2 tablespoons for garnish
    (optional)
Freshly ground white pepper

1. In large covered saucepan, bring 3 quarts water and 1 tablespoon salt to a boil over high heat.
2. While water is coming to a boil, fill large bowl with cold water. Under cold running water, rinse potatoes and peel with vegetable peeler, placing each one in bowl of water when finished.
3. Remove one potato from water. With chef's knife, cut potato widthwise into ⅛- to ¼-inch-thick slices. Return slices to water and repeat process with remaining potatoes.
4. In colander, drain potatoes and slip them carefully into boiling water. Cook over medium-high heat until slices can be easily penetrated with tip of knife, about 5 minutes.
5. In colander, drain potatoes, taking care not to break slices. With wooden spoon, carefully return potatoes to pan. Place a folded clean dish towel over pan and lay saucepan cover on top of it. With heat turned off, let potatoes sit in pan 5 minutes.
6. Transfer potatoes to large bowl and season with salt and pepper to taste. Leave potatoes to cool about 15 minutes.
7. While potatoes are cooling, combine mayonnaise, sour cream, and ¼ cup chives in small bowl, and stir with fork until blended. Cover and refrigerate.
8. Cover and refrigerate potatoes until needed.
9. Remove dressing and potatoes from refrigerator. With wooden spoon, spoon dressing over potatoes and gently toss to combine, being careful not to break potato slices.
10. Turn potatoes into serving dish and, if desired, garnish with chives.

Mushroom and Cauliflower Salad

Salt
Small head cauliflower (1 to 1½ pounds)
½ pound mushrooms
2 bunches celery
1 fresh chili pepper (optional)
½ cup olive oil
¼ cup tarragon wine vinegar
Freshly ground white pepper

1. In medium-size covered saucepan, bring 2 quarts water and 2 teaspoons salt to a boil.
2. While water is coming to a boil, cut cauliflower into bite-size florets. Place florets in colander, rinse thoroughly under cold running water, and drain.
3. Add cauliflower to boiling water and blanch 2 minutes over high heat. In colander, drain cauliflower and immediately refresh under cold running water for 2 minutes. Drain florets and set aside.
4. Wipe mushrooms clean with damp paper towels. With chef's knife, cut mushrooms into ⅛-inch-thick slices.
5. Remove outer stalks from celery and set aside for another use. Wash celery hearts, drain, and pat dry with paper towels. With chef's knife, cut into ¼-inch-thick slices.
6. Wearing thin rubber gloves, cut off and discard top of chili, if using. With paring knife, split chili lengthwise and using tip of knife, remove seeds and membranes. Rinse under cold running water and pat dry with paper towels. With chef's knife, chop and set aside.
7. In salad bowl, combine oil, vinegar, chili if using, and salt and pepper to taste, and beat with fork until blended.
8. Add cauliflower, mushrooms, and celery, and toss gently but thoroughly to combine.

Barbecued Beef Kabobs
Tomatoes with Goat Cheese
Cucumber and Grapefruit Salad

Select informal tableware for beef kabobs garnished with sesame seeds, goat cheese-stuffed tomatoes, and mixed salad.

For this barbecue, prepare the accompanying salads while the cubes of beef for the kabobs marinate. This way, you can be outdoors with your guests at cooking time.

Skewering meat to make kabobs was probably a Middle Eastern invention. If you prefer rare meat, put the cubes on the skewer close together and check for doneness after about 8 minutes.

WHAT TO DRINK

This menu's fresh, bright flavors call for a light but flavorful red wine such as a young California Zinfandel.

SHOPPING LIST AND STAPLES

1½ pounds beef tenderloin, cut into 1¼-inch cubes
6 medium-size ripe Italian plum tomatoes (about 1 pound total weight)
2 large cucumbers
Medium-size red onion
16 shallots or white onions (about ¾ pound total weight)
1 clove garlic
1 bunch scallions or chives
1 bunch watercress
Medium-size bunch fresh rosemary, or 2 teaspoons dried

2 pink grapefruit, or 2 medium-size seedless oranges
Medium-size orange
10 to 12 ounces fresh soft goat cheese, such as *Caprini di Capra*, or ricotta or farmer cheese
1 cup olive oil
¼ cup sesame oil
2 tablespoons tarragon wine vinegar
¼ cup soy sauce
4 teaspoons sesame seeds
Salt and freshly ground black pepper

UTENSILS

Barbecue
Medium-size saucepan with cover
13 x 9-inch baking dish
Large bowl
Platter
Colander
Salad spinner (optional)
Measuring cups and spoons
Chef's knife
Paring knife
2 wooden spoons
Slotted spoon
Teaspoon or melon baller
Grater
4 metal barbecue skewers, preferably flat
Basting brush
Vegetable peeler

START-TO-FINISH STEPS

Thirty minutes ahead: Start barbecue.

1. Follow kabobs recipe steps 1 through 4.
2. Follow salad recipe steps 1 through 3.
3. Follow tomatoes recipe steps 1 through 3.
4. Follow kabobs recipe steps 5 through 7.
5. Follow tomatoes recipe step 4.
6. Five minutes before kabobs are done, follow tomatoes recipe step 5 and salad recipe step 4.
7. Follow kabobs recipe step 8 and serve with tomatoes and salad on the side.

RECIPES

Barbecued Beef Kabobs

1 tablespoon grated orange zest
1 teaspoon minced garlic
2 tablespoons chopped fresh rosemary leaves, or 2 teaspoons dried, crumbled
¼ cup sesame oil
¼ cup olive oil
¼ cup soy sauce
½ teaspoon freshly ground black pepper
16 shallots or white onions, peeled
1½ pounds beef tenderloin, cut into 1¼-inch cubes
4 teaspoons sesame seeds

1. In medium-size covered saucepan, bring 2 quarts water to a boil over high heat.
2. In baking dish, combine orange zest, garlic, rosemary, sesame oil, olive oil, soy sauce, and pepper.
3. Plunge unpeeled onions or shallots into boiling water and blanch 1 minute. In colander, immediately drain onions and refresh under cold running water.
4. Stir marinade ingredients to recombine. Add beef cubes and onions or shallots, and gently toss until coated. Cover with plastic wrap and marinate at least 20 minutes, stirring and turning occasionally.
5. Using slotted spoon, transfer beef and onions or shallots to platter. On skewers, alternate beef cubes and onions or shallots.
6. Set grill rack 5 to 6 inches from coals. Place skewers on rack and cook until beef is seared and brown, 2 to 3 minutes. Turn skewers and cook another 2 to 3 minutes.
7. Continue to cook meat, basting and turning frequently, 8 to 10 minutes for rare, 10 to 12 minutes for medium rare, and 12 to 16 minutes for well-done.
8. Sprinkle kabobs with sesame seeds and serve.

Tomatoes with Goat Cheese

1 bunch scallions or chives
6 medium-size ripe Italian plum tomatoes
10 to 12 ounces fresh soft goat cheese
½ cup olive oil
Freshly ground black pepper

1. Wash scallions or chives and pat dry. Trim off ends and chop enough to measure 2 tablespoons.
2. Wash tomatoes and pat dry. Core and halve tomatoes crosswise. If necessary, cut a small slice from rounded end of each half to enable half to stand upright.
3. With teaspoon or melon baller, carefully hollow out each tomato half, discarding seeds and pulp.
4. Fill tomato shells with cheese, mounding it slightly.
5. Drizzle olive oil over tomatoes, season with pepper to taste, and garnish with scallions or chives.

Cucumber and Grapefruit Salad

1 bunch watercress
2 pink grapefruit, or 2 medium-size seedless oranges
Medium-size red onion, peeled and thinly sliced
2 large cucumbers, peeled and thinly sliced
¼ cup olive oil
2 tablespoons tarragon wine vinegar
Salt and freshly ground black pepper

1. Wash watercress and dry in salad spinner or pat dry with paper towels. Trim off stem ends and discard.
2. Peel grapefruit or oranges. With paring knife, remove as much white pith as possible and cut crosswise into ¼-inch-thick rounds.
3. In large bowl, combine watercress, grapefruit or oranges, onion, and cucumbers. Cover and refrigerate.
4. Toss mixture, first with olive oil, and then with tarragon vinegar and salt and pepper to taste.

Grilled Stuffed Lamb Chops
Mixed Bean Salad
Cheese and Fruit Medallions

A serving tray for each guest is a convenient way to serve grilled stuffed lamb chops and bean salad. The goat cheese and fruit can be served either as dessert or, if you prefer, as a second salad.

For this backyard barbecue, prepare the bean salad and partially prepare the cheese and fruit medallions before grilling the lamb chops.

The grilled lamb chops, stuffed with a fragrant bread-crumb and herb mixture, make an elegant entrée. For variety, omit the bread crumbs altogether and use only herbs and mushrooms. For a different flavor, baste the chops with a combination of white wine and olive oil.

WHAT TO DRINK

For the lamb, serve a dry red wine. Try a California or Italian Merlot, or, for a French accent, a St. Emilion.

SHOPPING LIST AND STAPLES

Four 1½-inch-thick lamb chops (about 1½ to 2 pounds total weight), with pockets cut lengthwise for stuffing
⅓ pound green beans
⅓ pound snow peas
⅓ pound yellow (wax) beans
½ pound fresh lima beans, or 10-ounce package frozen
2 mushrooms
1 shallot
1 clove garlic (optional)
Small bunch scallions
Small bunch parsley
Small bunch rosemary
1 bunch mint (optional)
1 lime (optional)
2 seedless oranges (optional)
Large pink grapefruit or 2 tangerines or 3 clementines
Small pineapple
1 kiwi (optional)
½ pound goat cheese (Montrachet with ash or Bûcheron), or Corolle or farmer cheese
½ cup plus 1 tablespoon olive oil
¼ cup walnut oil
2 tablespoons red wine vinegar
2 slices white or French bread, up to 2 days old
Salt and freshly ground black pepper
2 tablespoons dry white wine

UTENSILS

Barbecue
Food processor or blender

Medium-size saucepan
Salad bowl
Small bowl
Colander
Measuring cups and spoons
Chef's knife
Paring knife
2 wooden spoons
Long-handled barbecue tongs
Rubber spatula
Whisk
Basting brush
4 small poultry skewers

START-TO-FINISH STEPS

1. Start barbecue, placing grill rack on lowest level.
2. Follow bean salad recipe steps 1 through 3.
3. While beans are blanching, follow medallions recipe step 1.
4. Follow bean salad recipe steps 4 through 6.
5. Follow lamb recipe steps 1 through 3.
6. Follow medallions recipe steps 2 through 4.
7. Follow lamb recipe steps 4 through 9 and serve with bean salad.
8. For dessert, follow medallions recipe step 5 and serve.

RECIPES

Grilled Stuffed Lamb Chops

2 slices white or French bread, up to 2 days old
Small bunch parsley
Small bunch rosemary
Small bunch scallions
2 mushrooms
1 clove garlic (optional)
2 tablespoons dry white wine
Salt and freshly ground black pepper
Four 1½-inch-thick lamb chops (about 1½ to 2 pounds
    total weight), with pockets cut lengthwise for stuffing
¼ cup plus 1 tablespoon olive oil

1. In food processor or blender, process enough bread to make ½ cup bread crumbs.
2. Wash parsley, rosemary, and scallions, and pat dry. Trim scallions. With chef's knife, chop enough parsley, rosemary, and scallions to measure ¼ cup combined.
3. Wipe mushrooms with damp paper towels and chop finely. Peel garlic, if using, and mince.
4. In small bowl, combine bread crumbs, herbs, mushrooms, wine, and garlic, if using, and toss to blend. Add salt and pepper to taste, and toss again.
5. Using teaspoon, insert about ¼ cup stuffing mixture into each lamb chop pocket. Secure each pocket with a small poultry skewer. Rub both sides of each chop with 1 tablespoon olive oil and a light sprinkling of salt and pepper.
6. When barbecue is ready, set grill rack about 4 inches

from coals. Place chops on rack and cook 3 to 5 minutes on one side, or until nicely browned.
7. Using long-handled tongs, turn chops and grill another 3 to 5 minutes, or until nicely browned.
8. Brush chops with remaining oil. Turning every few minutes to ensure even color, cook chops to desired degree of doneness, about 12 to 15 minutes for medium rare.
9. Transfer chops to platter and let rest 2 to 3 minutes.

Mixed Bean Salad

Salt
1 shallot
⅓ pound green beans
⅓ pound snow peas
⅓ pound yellow (wax) beans
½ cup fresh or frozen lima beans
2 tablespoons red wine vinegar
¼ cup walnut oil
Freshly ground pepper

1. In medium-size covered saucepan, bring 2 quarts water and 2 teaspoons salt to a boil. Peel and mince shallot.
2. While water is coming to a boil, rinse and drain beans in colander. Remove stems from beans and discard.
3. Add beans to boiling water and blanch 1½ to 2 minutes.
4. In colander, drain beans and immediately refresh under cold running water for 2 minutes. Set aside.
5. In salad bowl, combine shallot, vinegar, oil, and salt and pepper to taste, and whisk until blended.
6. Add beans to salad bowl. With wooden spoon, toss gently to coat with dressing.

Cheese and Fruit Medallions

Lime wedges for garnish (optional)
1 bunch mint for garnish (optional)
Large pink grapefruit or 2 tangerines or 3 clementines
2 seedless oranges (optional)
Small pineapple
1 kiwi (optional)
½ pound goat cheese (Montrachet with ash or Bûcheron),
    or Corolle or farmer cheese
¼ cup olive oil
Salt and freshly ground pepper

1. Slice lime into wedges, if using. Wash mint, pat dry, and separate into sprigs for garnish, if using.
2. With paring knife, peel citrus fruit, including oranges, if using, removing as much white pith as possible, and cut crosswise into ¼-inch-thick rounds.
3. With chef's knife, carefully peel pineapple. Using point of paring knife, remove eyes. Quarter pineapple and remove core. Cut into ¼-inch-thick slices. Peel kiwi and cut into ¼-inch-thick slices.
4. Cut cheese into ¼-inch slices. On 4 individual plates arrange fruit and cheese slices in an overlapping pattern.
5. Drizzle oil over fruit and cheese, and season with salt and pepper to taste. Garnish with lime wedges and fresh mint sprigs, if desired.

Victoria Fahey

MENU 1 (Left)
Eggplant Salad
Falafel
Hummus
Cucumber Salad

MENU 2
Glazed Ham
Picnic Bread with Assorted Cheeses
Apple-Apricot Chutney

MENU 3
Spinach and Potato Soup
Herbed Roast Turkey Legs
Pumpkin-Corn Muffins

Before Victoria Fahey became a professional cook, she studied art, and now she concentrates on meals with intense visual appeal as well as good taste. The Menu 1 picnic, with its Middle Eastern dishes—eggplant salad, *falafel*, *hummus*, pita bread, cucumber salad, and an assortment of condiments—is an example. Because the food is transported in and served from glass canning jars, all the vibrant colors and textures are readily visible. For this mix-and-match vegetarian meal, your guests can vary both the fillings and the condiments to suit their tastes.

Although she lives in the country, Victoria Fahey has ready access to San Francisco, with its fine restaurants, well-stocked groceries, and exotic marketplaces. Both environments influence her cooking style, and her meals incorporate both country and cosmopolitan elements. Menu 2 is an American version of an English "ploughman's lunch," an informal meal commonly served in pubs. It consists of ham, cheese, home-baked bread, and chutney, all eaten as an open-faced sandwich. If you wish, you can buy all the components for this meal from a delicatessen or supermarket.

Victoria Fahey describes Menu 3 as reminiscent of medieval fare: It is a substantial meal, meant to be eaten out of hand. The herbed turkey legs, served cold or at room temperature, are suitable for lunch on a cross-country ski trip, with the soup kept hot in a Thermos®, or for a beach picnic, with the soup served chilled.

Transport the makings for this picnic, except for the pita bread, in glass jars that can be lined up together so that the colors and textures of their contents make a pleasing pattern. Serve the pita bread halves in a wooden bowl.

Eggplant Salad
Falafel / Hummus
Cucumber Salad

Pita bread, when cut in half, is ideal for stuffing with a variety of fillings. For this picnic, the choices are *falafel*—a blend of ground chick-peas (garbanzo beans), flours, spices, and garlic—eggplant salad, and cucumber salad. *Hummus*, a thick paste, also contains garbanzo beans, but here they are puréed with lemon juice, garlic, and *tahini* (sesame paste). Use the hummus either as a topping or a filling.

WHAT TO DRINK

With this menu, serve either a California Chenin Blanc for white or an Italian Valpolicella for red.

SHOPPING LIST AND STAPLES

½ pound tomatoes, or 14-ounce can chopped tomatoes in purée
2 cucumbers (about 1½ pounds total weight)
½ pound eggplant
½ pound zucchini
½ pound yellow onions
2 medium-size red onions
Small bunch scallions
8 medium-size cloves garlic
Small bunch mint, or 1 teaspoon dried
Small bunch dill, or 1 teaspoon dried
2 lemons
½ pint plain yogurt
½ pound feta cheese
15½-ounce can chick-peas
15-ounce can tahini (sesame paste)
7½-ounce can Greek olives
2 cups peanut oil or other vegetable oil
¼ cup olive oil
1 tablespoon red wine vinegar
1 tablespoon white wine vinegar
1 dozen pita breads
10-ounce box falafel mix, or 6 ounces if buying in bulk
9-ounce box dark raisins
1½ teaspoons dried oregano
¼ teaspoon cinnamon
Salt and freshly ground pepper

UTENSILS

Food processor or blender
Small heavy-gauge saucepan
Large sauté pan or skillet, with cover
2 platters
3 medium-size bowls
2 small bowls
Colander
Sieve
Measuring cups and spoons
Chef's knife
Paring knife
Wooden spoon
Slotted spoon
Teaspoon
Grater
Juicer
Deep-fat thermometer (optional)
Vegetable peeler
10 canning jars or other carrying containers

START-TO-FINISH STEPS

1. Follow eggplant salad recipe steps 1 and 2.
2. Follow falafel recipe steps 1 through 5.
3. While falafel balls are frying, follow eggplant salad recipe step 3.
4. Follow falafel recipe step 6.
5. Follow eggplant salad recipe steps 4 through 6.
6. While eggplant and zucchini are sautéing, follow hummus recipe steps 1 through 3.
7. Follow eggplant salad recipe step 7.
8. While eggplant mixture is simmering, peel garlic, mince, and follow cucumber salad recipe steps 1 and 2. Prepare condiments.
9. Follow eggplant salad recipe steps 8 and 9.
10. While eggplant is cooling, pack hummus, cucumber salad, falafel, scallions, red onions, raisins, yogurt, feta, and olives into individual canning jars or other carrying containers.
11. Follow eggplant salad recipe step 10.

RECIPES

Eggplant Salad

½ pound eggplant
½ pound zucchini
1½ teaspoons salt, approximately
½ pound yellow onions
3 cloves garlic

¼ cup olive oil
½ pound tomatoes or 14-ounce can chopped tomatoes
in purée
1½ teaspoons dried oregano
¼ teaspoon cinnamon
1 tablespoon red wine vinegar
Freshly ground pepper
1 dozen pita breads

1. Wash eggplant and zucchini, and pat dry with paper towels. With chef's knife, cut eggplant lengthwise into ⅛- to ¼-inch-thick slices and then into ⅛- to ¼-inch-thick strips. Cut strips crosswise into ⅛- to ¼-inch cubes. Place cubes in medium-size bowl. In same manner, prepare zucchini and add to eggplant.
2. Sprinkle vegetable cubes with 1½ teaspoons salt and toss until evenly coated. Turn cubes into colander set over same bowl and set aside.
3. Peel onions and garlic, and chop in food processor or with chef's knife. In sauté pan or skillet, heat 2 table-spoons olive oil over medium heat. Add onions and garlic, and sauté, stirring frequently, until softened and translu-cent, about 4 to 5 minutes. With slotted spoon, transfer to small bowl and reserve, leaving remaining oil in pan.
4. If using fresh tomatoes, wash, dry, and coarsely chop in food processor or with chef's knife.
5. With paper towels, pat dry eggplant and zucchini.
6. Add remaining 2 tablespoons oil to sauté pan and heat over medium-high heat 30 seconds. Add eggplant and zucchini cubes, and sauté, stirring frequently with wooden spoon, until cubes are heated through and have softened slightly, about 5 minutes.
7. Add reserved onions, garlic, and tomatoes to pan and stir to combine. Stir in oregano and cinnamon, cover pan, reduce heat to low, and simmer gently 15 minutes, stirring occasionally with wooden spoon.
8. Remove cover. If any liquid remains in pan, bring it to simmer over medium-high heat and watching carefully to be sure mixture does not burn, simmer, stirring occasion-ally, until excess liquid evaporates.
9. Remove pan from heat, add red wine vinegar and salt and pepper to taste, and stir to combine. Allow mixture to cool at least 15 minutes.
10. Cut pita breads in half, wrap in foil, and pack with eggplant.

Falafel

2 cups peanut or other vegetable oil
1 cup falafel mix

1. In small heavy-gauge saucepan, heat oil gradually over medium-low heat just until oil is warm, about 3 minutes.
2. Meanwhile, combine falafel mix with ¾ cup cup cold water in medium-size bowl. With wooden spoon, stir to blend.
3. Turn heat under oil to medium and heat oil until it registers 350 degrees on deep-fat thermometer or until a cube of bread browns in about 60 seconds.

4. Moisten your hands with cold water and form heaping teaspoon-size balls of falafel, rewetting your hands as necessary. Lay balls on platter as you finish them and keep forming balls until mixture is used up.
5. Fry falafel balls in 2 batches, 8 to 10 at a time, for 2 to 3 minutes, or until crisp and golden brown.
6. As they are finished, transfer them with a slotted spoon to paper-towel-lined platter to drain. Allow to cool.

Hummus

2 cups canned chick-peas, drained
4 medium-size cloves garlic
¼ cup lemon juice
½ cup tahini (sesame paste)
2½ teaspoons salt

1. Place chick-peas in sieve and rinse thoroughly under cold running water. Drain.
2. Peel garlic.
3. In food processor bowl or blender jar, combine chick-peas, garlic, lemon juice, tahini, and salt and purée until consistency is to your liking—hummus may be left slightly chunky or puréed to a smooth paste.

Cucumber Salad

2 cucumbers (about 1½ pounds total weight)
1 tablespoon white wine vinegar
2 tablespoons lemon juice
½ teaspoon minced garlic
1 tablespoon chopped fresh dill, or 1 teaspoon dried
1 tablespoon chopped fresh mint, or 1 teaspoon dried
Salt

1. Peel cucumbers and halve lengthwise. With teaspoon, seed each half. Discard seeds. Using food processor or chef's knife, cut cucumber into ⅛-inch dice.
2. Place cucumbers in medium-size bowl. Add vinegar and lemon juice, and toss until evenly coated. Add garlic and herbs, and toss to combine. Add salt to taste and toss.

Condiments

Small bunch scallions
2 medium-size red onions
1 cup dark raisins
½ pound feta cheese
1 cup plain yogurt
7½-ounce can Greek olives

1. Wash scallions and pat dry with paper towels. With chef's knife, slice into ⅛- to ¼-inch slices.
2. Peel onions and cut into ⅛- to ¼-inch slices.
3. Place raisins in sieve and rinse under cold water. Shake sieve to drain.
4. With your fingers, crumble feta into pea-size bits.
5. In small bowl, beat yogurt with a fork to smooth consistency.
6. Drain olives, reserving brine for any leftovers that may need to be stored.

Glazed Ham
Picnic Bread with Assorted Cheeses
Apple-Apricot Chutney

This picnic is well suited for a leisurely afternoon lunch in the woods or at the beach. The addition of ham makes it substantial enough for dinner. Prepare it far enough in advance to allow the bread to cool before cutting. At your picnic site, assemble your sandwiches open faced, as the English sometimes do, or, if you prefer, prepare them American style, between two slices of bread.

In spite of its short kneading time and rapid single rise, the bread has a dense texture. Follow the directions care-

For this rustic picnic, arrange the cheeses on a cutting board or platter and the ham on a separate plate. Serve the chutney and the optional pickled onions in individual bowls. If desired, bring beer along in a basket.

fully because timing is important in order to mix and bake the bread in under an hour. To ensure quick rising, let the dough rest in a warm place, such as the top of the preheated oven. Test the oven top with your hand: It is just right if you can rest your hand comfortably on its surface. If the dough is too cool, it will not rise quickly enough, and if it is too hot, the yeast will be killed.

The ham cooks with one of two mustard-based glazes. The first calls for dry English mustard, a powder that when reconstituted ranges from hot to very hot in flavor. The second calls for either Dijon mustard or sweet Scandinavian-style mustard.

English Farmhouse Cheddar is the traditional cheese for this English pub lunch. The rind of this cheese is gray-brown, and its interior is pale yellow. It has a firm

texture, nutty aroma, and a rich, mellow yet slightly sharp taste. If you wish, try other English cheeses such as Farmhouse Cheshire or Farmhouse Lancashire, or Double Gloucester, Cotswold (a Double Lancashire with chives and onions), Stilton (an English blue cheese), or Blue Cheshire. If you cannot find any of these English cheeses at your cheese shop or specialty food store, serve American Cheddar or Monterey Jack.

WHAT TO DRINK

The cook suggests either assorted English beers, gin and tonic, or English cider to accompany these dishes.

SHOPPING LIST AND STAPLES

1- to 2-pound canned ham
1 pound tart cooking apples, preferably Granny Smith, Pippin, or Gravenstein
Small onion (about 4 ounces)
2 medium-size cloves garlic
1 egg (optional)
1 stick plus 2 teaspoons unsalted butter
1½ to 2 pounds English cheese (Cheddar, Stilton, Cheshire, etc.) or American Cheddar or Monterey Jack
¼ cup apple cider vinegar

1 tablespoon Dijon mustard or Scandinavian-style prepared mustard (for Glaze 2)
10-ounce jar apricot, peach, nectarine, cherry, pineapple, or apple jam (without seeds or large chunks) or jelly (for Glaze 1)
8-ounce box dried apricots
15-ounce box golden raisins
2½ cups unbleached white flour plus 1 teaspoon
2 packets dry yeast
1 cup dark brown sugar, approximately
½ teaspoon granulated sugar
1 ounce crystallized ginger
1 teaspoon dry English mustard (for Glaze 1)
1 teaspoon whole mustard seeds
½ teaspoon ground cumin
½ teaspoon cinnamon
Salt

UTENSILS

Food processor (optional)
Medium-size saucepan with cover
Small saucepan
15 x 12-inch cookie sheet
18-inch jelly-roll pan or roasting pan
Rack that fits on jelly roll pan

Cooling rack
Large mixing bowl (if not using processor)
Small bowl plus one additional (if using egg glaze
    for bread)
Measuring cups and spoons
Chef's knife
Paring knife
Wooden spoon
Flour sifter
Apple corer (optional)
Pastry brush (if using egg glaze for bread)
Thermometer
Single-edge razor blade (optional)
Kitchen string
Jar with lid or other carrying container

START-TO-FINISH STEPS

1. Sift and measure flour, measure 1½ tablespoons yeast, and follow bread recipe steps 1 through 6.
2. While bread is rising, follow ham recipe steps 1 through 8.
3. While ham is glazing, peel and chop onion and garlic, and chop dried apricots and ginger for chutney recipe.
4. Remove ham from broiler and lower oven temperature to 450 degrees. Follow chutney recipe steps 1 through 4.
5. While chutney is cooking, follow bread recipe steps 7 through 9.
6. Follow chutney recipe steps 5 and 6.
7. Follow bread recipe step 10.
8. Follow ham recipe step 9 and bread recipe step 11.

RECIPES

Glazed Ham

1- to 2- pound canned ham

Glaze 1:
⅓ cup firmly packed dark brown sugar
1 teaspoon dry English mustard
2 tablespoons apricot, peach, nectarine, cherry, pine-
    apple, or apple jam (without seeds or large chunks)
    or jelly
1 teaspoon white flour

Glaze 2:
⅓ cup firmly packed dark brown sugar
1 tablespoon Dijon or Scandinavian-style
    prepared mustard
1 teaspoon white flour

1. Preheat broiler. Set broiler rack 6 to 8 inches below heating element.
2. Open can and with your hands lift out ham. Under cold running water, rinse off any meat jelly. Pat ham dry with paper towels.
3. With chef's knife, cut ham into ⅛- to ¼-inch-thick slices. (You should get about 12 from a 1-pound ham and 24 from a 2-pound ham.)
4. Pass a 1-foot-long piece of kitchen string lengthwise around ham, tying the ham slices so the shape of the ham is reconstructed and the slices are held together.
5. In a small bowl, combine ingredients for glaze of your choice and stir until blended.
6. Place ham on rack. With your fingers, rub ham with glaze, distributing any extra glaze on top.
7. Line jelly-roll pan or roasting pan with heavy-duty foil. Place rack with ham in pan and place pan on broiler rack.
8. Broil ham 3 to 5 minutes, or until glaze is bubbling and beginning to brown. Remove ham from broiler and allow to cool.
9. When ham is cool, wrap securely in heavy-duty aluminum foil.

Picnic Bread with Assorted Cheeses

1½ tablespoons dry yeast
½ teaspoon granulated sugar
2½ cups sifted unbleached white flour
1½ teaspoons salt
1 stick plus 2 teaspoons unsalted butter
1 egg (optional)
1½ to 2 pounds English cheese (Cheddar, Stilton, or
    Cheshire) or American Cheddar or Monterey Jack

1. In small saucepan, heat 1 cup water to between 105 and 115 degrees. The temperature must not be lower or higher.
2. In food processor fitted with metal blade or in large mixing bowl, combine water, yeast, and sugar.
3. When yeast starts to bubble to surface of water, about 2 to 5 minutes, add 2¼ cups flour and salt. Pulse food processor just until mixture forms a ball around blade, about 10 seconds. Or, in mixing bowl, quickly work dough together with your hands just until it forms a mass and cleans the sides of bowl.
4. Lightly flour cutting board with 1 tablespoon of remaining flour. Turn dough onto board and knead 2 minutes, gradually adding more flour if dough is too sticky. Shape dough into ball.

5. Grease cookie sheet with 2 teaspoons butter. Place dough on cookie sheet and pat into 7-inch circle. Cover with folded towel.

6. With palm of your hand, feel hot stove top until you find a place you can rest your hand without having to pull it away. If stove top is too hot, set large bowl on chair or kitchen stool placed near stove. Set cookie sheet with dough on bowl and let dough rise until doubled in bulk, about 30 minutes.

7. With chef's knife or single-edge razor blade, cut a shallow cross in top of loaf. (Cutting instrument must be very sharp.)

8. If desired, make an egg glaze for the bread: In small bowl, beat egg with 1 tablespoon cold water just until blended. With pastry brush, lightly paint bread with glaze, reserving remainder of glaze for later use.

9. Place bread in 450-degree oven. Immediately, reduce temperature to 400 degrees and bake bread 20 minutes, painting with remaining glaze, if using, once or twice more during baking. Bread is done when crust is golden brown and bread sounds hollow when you rap bottom with your fist.

10. Remove loaf from oven and place on rack to cool at least 30 minutes before wrapping in foil.

11. Wrap butter and cheese accompaniments.

Apple-Apricot Chutney

1 pound tart cooking apples, preferably Granny Smith, Pippin, or Gravenstein
½ cup finely chopped dried apricots
½ cup golden raisins
1 cup chopped onion
1 teaspoon chopped garlic
3 tablespoons chopped crystallized ginger
½ cup firmly packed dark brown sugar
¼ cup apple cider vinegar
1 teaspoon whole mustard seeds
½ teaspoon ground cumin
½ teaspoon cinnamon

1. Wash apples under cold running water and dry with paper towels. Do not peel. With chef's knife, cut apples in half. With paring knife or corer, core apples.

2. Place each half, flesh side down, on cutting board. With chef's knife held parallel to board and pressing your fingertips against the dome of the apple, cut through apple from stem end to root end, making ¼- to ½-inch-thick slices.

Turn knife so that blade is perpendicular to board and cut lengthwise through apple, making ¼- to ½-inch-wide strips. Holding knife perpendicular to board, cut apple crosswise into ¼- to ½-inch dice. Repeat with remaining apple halves. Transfer diced apples to medium-size saucepan.

3. Add remaining ingredients to apples and stir to combine.

4. Heat mixture over high heat until it begins to bubble. Reduce heat to medium-low, cover pan, and simmer gently 15 minutes.

5. Remove cover, raise heat to medium and continue to cook, stirring frequently with wooden spoon and watching carefully to prevent burning, until excess liquid has evaporated and mixture is thick and dark-colored, about 5 minutes.

6. Remove pan from heat and allow chutney to cool at least 30 minutes before transferring to glass jar with lid or other carrying container. If desired, chill container in refrigerator before packing.

ADDED TOUCH

A simple-to-prepare whole-wheat shortbread makes an ideal portable dessert to accompany this picnic.

Whole-Wheat Shortbread

2 sticks unsalted butter, softened
½ cup firmly packed light brown sugar
2½ cups sifted whole-wheat flour, approximately

1. Preheat oven to 350 degrees.

2. In large mixing bowl, combine butter and sugar, and beat with electric mixer at high speed until light and fluffy, about 2 to 3 minutes.

3. Turn speed to low and gradually add flour, beating until smooth and completely incorporated.

4. Lightly flour cutting or pastry board. Turn dough out onto board and roll into 8 x 8-inch square.

5. With chef's knife cut square into thirds lengthwise and crosswise, and then diagonally into 18 triangles. With fork, prick each triangle in three or four places.

6. Butter 12 x 9-inch baking sheet. With metal spatula, lift up triangles and arrange on baking sheet about ½ inch apart.

7. Place shortbread in oven and bake 25 to 30 minutes, or just until edges of triangles begin to brown. Transfer to rack and cool.

Spinach and Potato Soup
Herbed Roast Turkey Legs
Pumpkin-Corn Muffins

For convenience, serve this picnic on individual trays. Put the turkey legs and pumpkin-corn muffins on dinner plates, and pour the spinach and potato soup into bowls and garnish with lemon slices.

This adaptable picnic menu can be eaten at home or away from home and served warm in autumn or winter, or cold in summertime.

Turkey cut into parts is now readily available year-round in most supermarkets. Just before roasting, season each leg with *herbes du Provence*, a traditional blend of the herbs of southern France, usually including basil, savory, thyme, fennel, rosemary, and lavender. You can buy this herb mixture in specialty food stores, or substitute a standard poultry-seasoning blend. The turkey legs are roasted over a pan of hot water so that the steam cooks them quickly and prevents the meat from drying out. Cranberry or lingonberry sauce is an optional accompaniment to the turkey. Lingonberries are wild Scandinavian berries with a slightly piney taste.

When you prepare the soup for this picnic, carefully rinse the spinach in cold water several times to remove any particles of sand. Serve the soup hot or cold, depending on the season.

For the muffins, use unseasoned pumpkin purée, not a pumpkin-pie mixture, and serve them with sweet butter.

WHAT TO DRINK

The delicate flavors of this menu call for a simple white wine. Try either an Italian Soave or a German Riesling.

SHOPPING LIST AND STAPLES

4 turkey legs (1 to 1½ pounds each)
1 pound baking potatoes
¾ pound spinach
1 bunch leeks (about 1 pound), or ¼ pound
    yellow onions
Small bunch fresh tarragon, or 1 teaspoon dried
3 medium-size cloves garlic
1 lemon plus additional lemon (optional)
1 orange
8-ounce can cranberry or 10-ounce can lingonberry
    sauce (optional)
3 eggs
⅔ cup milk
½ pint light cream or half-and-half
2 sticks unsalted butter
16-ounce can pumpkin purée
3 cups chicken stock, preferably homemade
    (page 13), or canned

1 cup unbleached white flour
⅔ cup cornmeal
½ cup firmly packed light brown sugar
1 tablespoon baking powder
3 tablespoons *herbes du Provence,* or 1 tablespoon
    poultry seasoning
1 teaspoon cinnamon
½ teaspoon nutmeg
Salt and freshly ground black pepper
1 teaspoon freshly ground white pepper

UTENSILS

Food processor or blender
Large saucepan with cover
Small saucepan
12 x 9-inch jelly-roll pan or roasting pan
Rack to fit jelly-roll pan
Cooling rack
12-cup 2½ inch muffin tin
Large mixing bowl (if not using processor) plus
    additional bowl if chilling soup
Medium-size bowl
2 small bowls
Colander
Flour sifter
Measuring cups and spoons
Chef's knife
Paring knife
Wooden spoon
Rubber spatula
Whisk
Electric mixer (if not using processor)
Grater
Basting brush
Vegetable peeler
Cake tester or toothpick
Thermos® or cooler
2 carrying containers for berry sauce and butter

START-TO-FINISH STEPS

One hour ahead: Remove turkey legs from refrigerator
and allow to come to room temperature.

1. Preheat oven to 450 degrees, placing one rack in lowest
position and one rack at middle level.
2. Follow turkey legs recipe steps 1 through 5.
3. While turkey legs are roasting, follow soup recipe steps
1 through 6.
4. While potatoes are cooking, chop tarragon, squeeze
lemon juice, and slice lemons for garnish, if using. Sift
flour for muffins recipe.
5. Follow soup recipe steps 7 through 10 and set aside,
partially covered.
6. Grate orange rind and follow muffins recipe steps 1
through 4.
7. If serving soup chilled, follow soup recipe step 11.

8. Fifteen minutes before turkey legs are done, follow
muffins recipe step 5.
9. Follow turkey legs recipe step 6 and muffins recipe
step 6.
10. If serving soup hot, 5 minutes before packing turkey
and muffins, follow soup recipe step 12.
11. Follow turkey recipe step 7, soup recipe step 13, and
pack turkey legs and muffins.

RECIPES

Spinach and Potato Soup

1 bunch leeks (about 1 pound) or ¼ pound yellow onions
3 medium-size cloves garlic
4 tablespoons unsalted butter
1 pound baking potatoes
3 cups chicken stock
¾ pound spinach
1 tablespoon chopped fresh tarragon, or 1 teaspoon dried
2 tablespoons lemon juice
1 teaspoon freshly ground white pepper
½ cup light cream or half-and-half
Salt
8 lemon slices for garnish (optional)

1. With chef's knife, trim leeks, removing roots and green
tops. Split leeks in half lengthwise and wash under cold
running water, making sure water runs between layers
and flushes out sand. Pat dry with paper towels. With
chef's knife, chop leeks into ¼-inch pieces. If using onions,
peel and chop.
2. Peel garlic and coarsely chop.
3. In large saucepan, melt butter over medium heat. Add
leeks and garlic, and sauté, stirring frequently with
wooden spoon, until leeks become transparent, about 5
minutes.
4. Fill medium-size bowl with cold water. With vegetable
peeler, or sharp paring knife, peel potatoes and, to prevent discoloring, drop each one into bowl of water as it is
peeled.
5. With chef's knife, cut potatoes into ½-inch cubes.
6. To saucepan with leeks, add cubed potatoes and stock.
Raise heat to high and bring to a boil. Reduce heat to
medium-low, cover, and simmer until potatoes are tender
when pierced with tip of knife, about 10 minutes.
7. With chef's knife, trim off spinach roots and lower stems
and discard. Place spinach in colander and wash thoroughly under cold running water. Shake colander to drain
off excess water.
8. Gather leaves in several bunches and place on cutting
board. With chef's knife, chop each bunch coarsely into
bite-size pieces. Add spinach all at once to simmering soup
and cook 2 minutes, or just until spinach has wilted.
9. Add tarragon, lemon juice, white pepper, and cream or
half-and-half, and stir with wooden spoon until combined.
Add salt to taste and stir again.
10. Transfer soup to bowl of food processor or blender jar
and purée. If using blender, purée in several batches and

hold lid down tightly when you turn machine on. Transfer soup to medium-size bowl.

11. If serving soup chilled, fill large bowl with crushed ice or ice water and set soup bowl in it. With whisk, stir soup frequently until chilled, 10 to 15 minutes.

12. If serving soup hot, return soup to saucepan and bring just to a simmer, stirring with whisk, over medium heat.

13. Transfer soup to Thermos®. Serve garnished with lemon slices, if desired.

Herbed Roast Turkey Legs

4 tablespoons unsalted butter
3 tablespoons *herbes du Provence*, or 1 tablespoon poultry seasoning
1 tablespoon salt
1 teaspoon freshly ground black pepper
4 turkey legs (1 to 1½ pounds each)
8-ounce can cranberry or 10-ounce can lingonberry sauce (optional)

1. In small saucepan, melt butter over low heat. Remove pan from heat.

2. In small bowl, combine herbs or poultry seasoning with salt and pepper, and stir with fork until blended.

3. Loosen skin on turkey leg by slipping your fingers under it. Pull skin back but don't detach and, pushing herb mixture as far under skin as possible, rub flesh with it, using 1 tablespoon of herb mixture per turkey leg. Pull skin back into place.

4. Line a jelly-roll pan or roasting pan with heavy-duty aluminum foil and place rack on it. Arrange turkey legs on rack. Using basting brush, baste legs with melted butter.

5. Place pan on middle shelf of preheated 450-degree oven. Pour 2 cups very hot tap water around rack in roasting pan. Roast legs 50 minutes if they weigh 1 pound each, 1 hour and 5 minutes if they weigh 1½ pounds each, or until juices run clear when legs are pierced with knife tip.

6. Remove from oven and cool at least 20 minutes before wrapping in heavy-duty aluminum foil.

7. Turn cranberry or lingonberry sauce, if using, into carrying container with lid.

Pumpkin-Corn Muffins

1 cup sifted unbleached white flour
1 tablespoon baking powder
1 teaspoon cinnamon
½ teaspoon nutmeg
1½ teaspoons salt
⅔ cup cornmeal
½ cup firmly packed light brown sugar
1 stick unsalted butter, approximately
3 eggs
1 cup canned pumpkin purée
⅔ cup milk
1½ tablespoons orange peel, finely grated

1. Butter 12-cup 2½-inch muffin tin.

2. In bowl of food processor or in large mixing bowl, combine flour, baking powder, cinnamon, nutmeg, salt, cornmeal, and brown sugar. If using processor, add butter and process 10 seconds. If using electric mixer, first stir dry ingredients together with fork, then add butter and beat with mixer at low and then medium speed until ingredients are blended.

3. Break eggs into small bowl and, with fork, beat lightly. If using processor, add eggs, pumpkin purée, milk, and orange peel to flour-butter mixture and process 5 to 10 seconds or until blended. With rubber spatula, scrape down sides of bowl, if necessary, and blend another 2 or 3 seconds. If using electric mixer, add ingredients to bowl one at a time, beating well after each addition.

4. Spoon batter into buttered muffin tin, filling cups two-thirds full.

5. Place muffin tin on lower shelf of preheated 450-degree oven and bake 10 to 15 minutes, or until muffins have puffed and browned and a cake tester or toothpick inserted into center comes out clean.

6. Remove muffins from tin immediately, set on rack, and let cool at least 20 minutes before wrapping in foil.

ADDED TOUCH

This custardy dessert resembles a standard rice pudding, but the wild rice gives the pudding a slightly chewy texture and a subtle nutty taste. Covering the pudding with foil during baking is important to keep it from drying out. On a hot day, pack the cooled pudding in a sealed container in an ice chest.

Wild Rice Pudding

1 cup wild rice (about 6 ounces)
3 eggs
¾ cup pure maple syrup, or ½ cup light brown sugar, firmly packed
1 teaspoon ginger
½ teaspoon nutmeg
¼ teaspoon salt
1 cup milk
½ cup dark raisins (optional)

1. In medium-size saucepan, bring 3 cups of water to a boil.

2. Place rice in sieve and rinse thoroughly under cold running water. Drain rice and add to boiling water, stirring once. Reduce to a gentle simmer, cover pan, and cook until tender, about 60 minutes. Let cool 5 to 10 minutes.

3. Meanwhile, preheat oven to 325 degrees.

4. Break eggs into 1-quart ovenproof bowl and beat lightly with fork. Add syrup or brown sugar and spices, and stir until blended. Add milk and raisins, if desired, and stir to combine.

5. Add rice to egg mixture and stir with fork to combine thoroughly. Cover bowl with aluminum foil.

6. Place bowl in deep baking pan and add hot water to reach halfway up sides of bowl.

7. Place pan and bowl in oven and bake 45 minutes, or until pudding has set.

Acknowledgments

Special thanks are due to Janet Bartucci, Myers Communi/Counsel, Inc., for her assistance in the preparation of this volume.

The Editors would also like to thank the following for their courtesy in lending items for photography: *Cover*: fork, platters—Dean & DeLuca; tongs—Broadway Panhandler. *Frontispiece*: Utensils, paper plates, baskets—Broadway Pandhandler; napkins in bread basket—Fabindia, courtesy of Primitive Artisans; napkins with fruit—Pierre Deux. *Pages 20–21*: flatware—The Lauffer Company; containers—Pottery Barn. *Page 24*: plates, mat—Pottery Barn. *Page 26*: salad plate—Eigen Arts; napkins, paper plates—Marimekko; platter, bowls—Pottery Barn. *Pages 28–29*: napkins—Fabindia, courtesy of Primitive Artisans; tray, dinner plate—Pottery Barn. *Page 32*: flatware—The Lauffer Company; salad bowl and servers—Pottery Barn; linens—Mosseri. *Page 34*: cloth in basket—Asta Cloth; cloth and napkins—La Jacquard Française; basket—L. L. Bean; plates—Pottery Barn. *Pages 36–37*: baskets, napkins—Urban Outfitters; casseroles, servers—Dean & DeLuca; plates, glasses, knives—Wolfman-Gold & Good Company; duck casserole, blanket—Barney's Chelsea Passage. *Page 40*: board, platters, rug—Pat Guthman Antiques, Southport, CT. *Pages 44–45*: platter—Pottery Barn; seviche bowl—Barney's Chelsea Passage; basket, servers—Urban Outfitters; napkin—Mosseri. *Pages 48–49*: board—Pottery Barn; flatware—

Conran's; cloth—Barney's Chelsea Passage; napkin around wine—Fabindia, courtesy of Primitive Artisans; knife—J.A. Henckels Zwillingswerk, Inc.; glasses, small basket—Urban Outfitters; napkins, large basket—Wolfman-Gold & Good Company; plates—Buffalo China. *Page 52*: flatware—Dean & DeLuca; plates—Barney's Chelsea Passage; blanket—Pottery Barn; tray—Wolfman-Gold & Good Company. *Page 54*: cloth—Laura Ashley; china—Haviland Limoges; napkin—Leacock & Company. *Pages 56–57*: bowls—Bennington Pottery; trays, plates, bowls, napkins—Pottery Barn. *Pages 60–61*: flatware—The Lauffer Company; baskets, plates—Pottery Barn; napkins, cloth—Mosseri. *Page 64*: containers, napkins, rug, basket—Pottery Barn. *Pages 66–67* (shot in Prospect Park, Brooklyn, NY): servers, black platters—Dean & DeLuca; basket—Hammacher Schlemmer; cloth—Ad Hoc Softwares. *Page 70* (shot in Sherwood Island, CT). *Page 72*: linens, plates, glasses—Pierre Deux; flatware—The Lauffer Company. *Pages 74–75*: flatware—The Lauffer Company; cloth—Fabindia, courtesy of Primitive Artisans; basket—Pierre Deux; serving bowl, glasses, plates—Pottery Barn; platters—Eigen Arts. *Page 78* (shot in Prospect Park, Brooklyn, NY): porcelain containers—Dean & DeLuca; large basket, blue napkins—Urban Outfitters; striped napkins, plates, blanket—Ad Hoc Housewares; insulated container—Ludwig Beck of Munich. *Pages 82–83*: blue bowl—Bennington Pottery; plat-

ters—Fiestaware. *Page 86*: glass—Urban Outfitters; plate—Claudia Schwide, courtesy of Barney's Chelsea Passage; cloth—Barney's Chelsea Passage. *Page 88*: flatware—The Lauffer Company. *Pages 90–91*: small checked napkins, cloth—Fabindia, courtesy of Primitive Artisans; large checked napkins—Broadway Panhandler. *Pages 94–95*: basket—L.L. Bean. *Page 98* (shot in Prospect Park, Brooklyn, NY): spoon—The Lauffer Company; napkin—Fabindia, courtesy of Primitive Artisans; tray—Wolfman-Gold & Good Company; plate—Urban Outfitters; bowl—Ad Hoc Housewares. *Kitchen equipment courtesy of*: White-Westinghouse, Commercial Aluminum Cookware Co., Robot-Coupe, Caloric, Kitchen-Aid, J.A. Henckels Zwillingswerk, Inc.

Illustrations by Ray Skibinski.
Production by Giga Communications

Mail-Order Sources for Mesquite

Laredo Industries
1919 Pennsylvania Avenue, Suite 505
Washington, D.C.   20006
(202) 293-0720

Bloomfield Farms, Inc.
175 South San Antonio Road
Los Altos, CA   94022
(415) 941-0410

Index

Anchovies, 16
apple
  and apricot chutney, 91, 94–97
  crumb pie, 43
apricot-apple chutney, 91, 94–97
artichokes
  oreganata, 48, 54–55
  stuffed with wild mushrooms and prosciutto, 63
arugula with tomato and onion salad, 40–42
asparagus with garlic dressing, 37–39

Bailey, Frank, 5
  menus of, 75–81
baking, 15
barbecued dishes
  beef kabobs, 82, 86–87
  bluefish with spinach, bread, and vegetable stuffing, 37, 40–42
  butterflied leg of lamb with savory sauce, 21, 24–25
  corn, 48–51

Cornish hens with Oriental flavors, 28–31
fajitas, 75, 78–79
grilled and baked fish, 75, 80–81
loin of lamb with tomato and mushroom stuffing, 66–69
marinated chicken breasts, 82–85
mesquite-grilled clams, oysters, and lobsters, 57–59
monkfish with lime-butter baste, 28, 32–33
Monterey beef roast, 21, 26–27
pork loin with garlic and sage, 48, 54–55
rabbit, 48, 52–53
roast potatoes with herbed butter, 26–27
salmon steaks with fresh dill and thyme, 66, 70–71
salmon with fennel, lemon, and onion, 48–51
shrimp with butter sauce, 75, 80–81
stuffed lamb chops, 82, 88–89

sweet-and-spicy spareribs, 37, 44–46
yellow and green bell peppers, grilled, 48, 52–53
barbecues
  defined, 7
  fire building, 11–12, 11 *illus.*
  firestarters, 11
  fuels, 10–11
  grills, 9–11, 10 *illus.*
  safety notes, 8
  tools, 14, 18
barbecuing techniques, 12–13
basil dip, creamy, with raw vegetables, 28, 34–35
basting, 12
Baxter, Nicholas, 5
  menus of, 66–73
bean, mixed, salad, 82, 88–89
beef
  barbecuing techniques, 12
  fajitas, 75, 78–79
  hamburgers, 28, 34–35
  kabobs, 82, 86–87
  roast, Monterey, 21, 26–27

bell pepper(s)
  roasted, with leeks and Bûcheron, 40–41, 43
  roasted, salad, 80–81
  with wild rice and cassis, 72–73
  yellow and green, grilled, 48, 52–53
Bermuda onions, 17
berry tart, 51
black bread, 47
black peppercorns, 16
blanching, 15
bluefish with spinach, bread, and vegetable stuffing, 37, 40–42
braising, 15
braziers, open, 10, 10 *illus.*
bread
  black, 47
  corn and pumpkin muffins, 98–100
  picnic, with assorted cheeses, 91, 94–97
bread crumbs, 17
briquettes, charcoal, 10, 11 *illus.*

broccoli and carrot salad, 26–27
Bûcheron and leeks with roasted pepper, 40–41, 43
bulgur with carrots and scallions, 32–33
butter, 17
  clarified, 15
  sautéing with, 15
butterflied leg of lamb with savory sauce, 21, 24–25

Cabbage
  Chinese, with snow peas and cucumber with curried mayonnaise, 21–23
  honey-mustard coleslaw, 44–47
cake, light chocolate, 71
capers, 16
carrots
  and broccoli salad, 26–27
  with new potatoes and scallions, herbed, 57–59
  and scallions with bulgur, 32–33
  with snow peas, stir-fried, 28–31
carrying containers, 9
cauliflower and mushroom salad, 82–85
charcoal briquettes, 10, 11 illus.
cheese, 17
  assorted, with picnic bread, 91, 94–97
  Bûcheron, with leeks and roasted pepper, 40–41, 43
  and fruit medallions, 82, 88–89
  goat, with tomatoes, 82, 86–87
  and pasta salad, 37–39
chicken
  breasts, marinated, 82–85
  with duck and veal, salad, 37–39
  and rice salad, Oriental, 21–23
chicken stock, 13, 17
chimney starters, 11
Chinese cabbage, snow peas, and cucumber with curried mayonnaise, 21–23
chocolate cake, light, 71
chutney, apple-apricot, 91, 94–97
clams, oysters, and lobsters, mesquite-grilled, 57–59
Cliborne, Bruce, 5
  menus of, 57–65
coleslaw, honey-mustard, 44–47
cookie cups, fresh fruit in, 28–31
cooking equipment, 18, 19, illus.
cooking safety, 8
cooking techniques
  barbecuing, 12–13
  basic, 13–15
coriander, orange, and radish salad, 57, 64–65
corn
  grilled, 48–51
  and pumpkin muffins, 98–100
  salad, marinated, 60–62
Cornish hens with Oriental flavors, 28–31
covered cookers, 10, 10 illus.

cucumber(s)
  with Chinese cabbage and snow peas with curried mayonnaise 21–23
  and grapefruit salad, 82, 86–87
  and radishes with watercress, 48–51
  salad, 91–93
  and tomatoes with lime, 57–59

Davis, Ron, 4
  menus of, 37–47
desserts
  apple crumb pie, 43
  berry tart, 51
  fruit in cookie cups, 28–31
  fruit layers with vanilla sauce, 35
  light chocolate cake, 71
  pineapple with orange-chocolate sauce, 21–23
  sweet-and-sour peaches and plums, 60–62
  whole-wheat shortbread, 97
  wild rice pudding, 100
direct barbecuing, 12
drinks, 15
drip pan, 12, 12 illus., 14
duck
  with chicken and veal, salad, 37–39
  orange, cold, 75–77

Eggplant salad, 91–93
eggs, 17
electric appliances, 18
electric firestarters, 11
electric grills, 11
equipment
  barbecue, 9–12, 9 illus., 10 illus., 12 illus., 18
  cooking, 18, 19 illus.
  picnic, 8–9, 18

Fahey, Victoria, 5
  menus of, 91–100
fajitas, 75, 78–79
falafel, 91–93
fennel, poached, 57
fire pits, 10
fires
  building of, 11–12, 11 illus.
  firestarters, 11
  flare-ups, prevention of, 12
  fuels, 10–11
  safety with, 8
fish
  barbecuing techniques, 13
  bluefish with spinach, bread, and vegetable stuffing, 37, 40–42
  grilled, baked, 75, 80–81
  monkfish with lime-butter baste, 28, 32–33
  salmon steaks with fresh dill and thyme, 66, 70–71
  salmon with fennel, lemon, and onion, 48–51
foil, 9, 9 illus.

foil-wrapped vegetables, 13
fruit
  berry tart, 51
  and cheese medallions, 82, 88–89
  in cookie cups, 28–31
  grapefruit and cucumber salad, 82, 86–87
  layers with vanilla sauce, 35
  orange, radish, and coriander salad, 57, 64–65
  pineapple with orange-chocolate sauce, 21–23
  sweet-and-sour peaches and plums, 60–62
fuels, 10–11

Garlic, 16
gas fuel, 11
gas grills, 11
ginger, fresh, 17
goat cheese with tomatoes, 82, 86–87
grapefruit and cucumber salad, 82, 86–87
green peppercorns, 16
green peppers, grilled, 48, 52–53
grills, 9–11, 10 illus.

Ham, glazed, 91, 94–96
hamburgers, 28, 34–35
  barbecuing technique, 12
  French, 35
  Mexican, 35
hazelnut and watercress salad, 66–69
herbed crème fraîche, sea scallops with, 57, 64–65
herbed new potatoes, carrots, and scallions, 57–59
herbed roast turkey legs, 91, 98–100
herbs, 16
honey-mustard coleslaw, 44–47
hummus, 91–93

Indirect barbecuing, 12
Italian onions, 17
Italian plum tomatoes, 17

Lamb
  barbecuing techniques, 13
  butterflied leg of, with savory sauce, 21, 24–25
  chops, stuffed, 82, 88–89
  loin, with tomato and mushroom stuffing, 66–69
  and vegetables, stir-fried, 25
  and vegetables with vinaigrette, 25
leeks, with roasted pepper and Bûcheron, 40–41, 43
lobsters, clams, and oysters, mesquite-grilled, 57–59

Marinades, 12
marinated chicken breasts, 82–85
marinated corn salad, 60–62
Mediterranean tomato salad, 48, 52–53

mesquite, 11
mesquite-grilled clams, oysters, and lobsters, 57–59
Mexican hamburgers, 35
Middle Eastern dishes
  cucumber salad, 91–93
  eggplant salad, 91–93
  falafel, 91–93
  hummus, 91–93
  mint, fresh, and watercress salad, 24–25
  monkfish with lime-butter baste, 28, 32–33
Monterey beef roast, 21, 26–27
muffins, pumpkin-corn, 98–100
mushrooms
  and cauliflower salad, 82–85
  and tomato, lamb loin stuffed with, 66–69
  wild, and prosciutto, artichokes stuffed with, 63
mustards, 17

New potatoes, 17
  with carrots and scallions, herbed, 57–59
nuts, 16

Oils, 16–17
  sautéing with, 15
olive oil, 16
onions, 17
  with tomato and arugula salad, 40–42
  orange, radish, and coriander salad, 57, 64–65
Oriental dishes
  chicken and rice salad, 21–23
  Cornish hens with Oriental flavors, 28–31
  stir-fried carrots with snow peas, 28–31
  stir-fried lamb and vegetables, 25
orzo with sour cream and black pepper, 66–69
oysters, clams, and lobsters, mesquite-grilled, 57–59

Packing picnics, 9, 9 illus.
pan grilling, 15
pantry, 16–17
parsley, 17
pasta
  salad with pesto, 75–77
  with three cheeses, 37–39
pâté, spinach, 75–77
peaches and plums, sweet-and-sour, 60–62
peas, snow, see snow peas
peppers, see bell peppers
perishables, 8
pesto with pasta salad, 75–77
picnic dishes
  chilled cream of tomato soup with tequila, 75, 78–79
  cold orange duck, 75–77
  corn and pumpkin muffins, 98–100
  desserts, see desserts

falafel, 91–93
glazed ham, 91, 94–96
grilled pork loin with fresh thyme, 57, 60–62
herbed roast turkey legs, 91, 98–100
hummus, 91–93
picnic bread with assorted cheeses, 91, 94–97
roast pork loin with garlic and sage, 48, 54–55
salad, *see* salad
scallop seviche, 37, 44–46
sea scallops with herbed crème fraîche, 57, 64–65
spinach and potato soup, 91, 98–100
veal loin poached with vegetables in white wine, 66, 72–73
vegetables, see names of vegetables; vegetables
see also barbecued dishes
picnics
defined, 7
equipment, 8–9, 18
history of, 7
packing, 9, 9 *illus.*
safety notes, 8
pie, apple crumb, 43
pineapple with orange-chocolate sauce, 21–23
plums and peaches, sweet-and-sour, 60–62
poaching, 15
pork
barbecuing techniques, 13
glazed ham, 91, 94–96
grilled loin, with fresh thyme, 57, 60–62
roast loin with garlic and sage, 48, 54–55
potatoes, 17
new, with carrots and scallions, herbed, 57–59
roast, with herbed butter, 26–27
salad Vichyssoise, 82–85
and spinach soup, 91, 98–100
poultry
barbecuing techniques, 13
cold orange duck, 75–77
Cornish hens with Oriental flavors, 28–31
duck, chicken, and veal salad, 37–39
herbed roast turkey legs, 91, 98–100
marinated chicken breasts, 82–85
Oriental chicken and rice salad, 21–23
prosciutto and wild mushrooms, artichokes stuffed with, 63
pumpkin-corn muffins, 91, 98–100

Rabbit
barbecuing techniques, 13
grilled, 48, 52–53

radishes
and cucumbers with watercress salad, 48–51
and orange with coriander salad, 57, 64–65
Rall, Roberta, 4
menus of, 28–35
red onions, 17
red pepper(s)
roasted, with leeks and Bûcheron, 40–41, 43
roasted, salad, 80–81
with wild rice and cassis, 72–73
rice, 17
and chicken salad, Oriental, 21–23
Spanish, salad, 75, 78–79
wild, pudding, 100
wild, with red pepper and cassis, 72–73
Risser, John, 5
menus of, 82–89
roasting, 15
Rock Cornish game hens with Oriental flavors, 28–31

Safety, 8
saffron, 16
salad
carrot and broccoli, 26–27
Chinese cabbage, snow peas, and cucumber with curried mayonnaise, 21
corn, marinated, 60–62
cucumber, 91–93
cucumber and grapegruit, 82, 86–87
cucumber and radishes with watercress, 48–51
cucumber and tomatoes with lime, 57–59
duck, chicken, and veal, 37–39
eggplant, 91–93
fresh mint and watercress, 24–25
honey-mustard coleslaw, 44–47
marinated vegetables, 32–33
Mediterranean tomato, 48, 52–53
mixed bean, 82, 88–89
mushroom and cauliflower, 82–85
orange, radish, and coriander, 57, 64–65
Oriental chicken and rice, 21–23
pasta with pesto, 75–77
pasta with three cheeses, 37–39
potato, Vichyssoise, 82–85
roasted pepper, 80–81
Spanish rice, 75, 78–79
tomato, onion, and arugula, 40–42
watercress and hazelnut, 66–69
salmon
with fennel, lemon, and onion, 48–51
steaks with fresh dill and thyme, 66, 70–71
sautéing, 14–15

scallions, 17
and carrots with bulgur, 32–33
with new potatoes and carrots, herbed, 57–59
scallops
sea, with herbed crème fraîche, 57, 64–65
seviche, 37, 44–46
sea scallops with herbed crème fraîche, 57, 64–65
sesame oil, 16–17
seviche, scallop, 37, 44–46
shallots, 17
shellfish
grilled shrimp with butter sauce, 75, 80–81
mesquite-grilled clams, oysters, and lobsters, 57–59
scallop seviche, 37, 44–46
sea scallops with herbed crème fraîche, 57, 64–65
sherry vinegar, 17
shortbread, whole-wheat, 97
shrimp grilled with butter sauce, 75, 80–81
skewered foods, 13
skewers, 14, 14 *illus.*
snow peas
with carrots, stir-fried, 28–31
with Chinese cabbage and cucumber with curried mayonnaise, 21–23
soup
chilled cream of tomato with tequila, 75, 78–79
spinach and potato, 91, 98–100
Spanish onions, 17
Spanish rice salad, 75, 78–79
spareribs, sweet-and-spicy, 37, 44–46
spices, 16
spinach
bluefish stuffed with, 37, 40–42
pâté, 75–77
and potato soup, 91, 98–100
squash, yellow, and zucchini, stir-fried, 24–25
steaks, barbecuing technique, 12
stir frying, 15
stock, chicken, 13, 17
stone barbecues, 10
sweet-and-sour peaches and plums, 60–62

Tabletop grills, 10, 10 *illus.*
tableware, 8
tapénade, 48, 54–55
tarragon vinegar, 17
tart, berry, 51
tequila, chilled cream of tomato soup with, 75, 78–79
thyme
and fresh dill with salmon steaks, 66, 70–71
with grilled pork lion, 57, 60–62
tomato(es), 17
and cucumbers with lime, 57–59
with goat cheese, 82, 86–87

Mediterranean salad, 48, 52–53
and mushroom stuffed loin of lamb, 66–69
with onion and arugula salad, 40–42
soup, chilled cream of, with tequila, 75, 78–79
tools, picnic, 9
turkey legs, herbed roast, 91, 98–100

Uetz, Jane, 4
menus of, 21–27

Veal
with duck and chicken, salad, 37–39
loin, poached with vegetables in white wine, 66, 72–73
vegetables
bluefish stuffed with, 37, 40–42
with duck, chicken, and veal, salad, 37–39
foil-wrapped, 13
and lamb, stir-fried, 25
and lamb with vinaigrette, 25
marinated, 32–33
mélange of, 66, 70–71
raw, with creamy basil dip, 28, 34–35
with veal loin poached in white wine, 66, 72–73
see also names of vegetables
vinegars, 17

Water chestnuts, 17
watercress
with cucumber and radish salad, 48–51
and fresh mint salad, 24–25
and hazelnut salad, 66–69
white onions, 17
white peppercorns, 16
whole-wheat shortbread, 97
wild rice
pudding, 100
with red pepper and cassis, 72–73
wines, 17
Wise, Victoria, 4
menus of, 48–55
wood for barbecuing, 11

Yellow onions, 17
yellow peppers, grilled, 48, 52–53
yellow squash and zucchini, stir-fried, 24–25

Zucchini and yellow squash, stir-fried, 24–25

Time-Life Books Inc. offers a wide range of fine recordings, including a Big Band series. For subscription information, call 1-800-621-7026, or write TIME-LIFE MUSIC, Time & Life Building, Chicago, Illinois 60611.